Little Kids Worship presents

D1606968

The

ABC's

of the Bible

Lisa Woodruff

NELSON IMPACT
A Division of Thomas Nelson Publishers
Since 1798

www.thomasnelson.com

Published by Nelson Impact, a Division of Thomas Nelson, Inc., P.O. Box 141000, Nashville, Tennessee, 37214.

Scripture quotations marked ICB are taken from the *International Children's Bible*®. Copyright © 1986, 1988 by Word Publishing, a Division of Thomas Nelson, Inc. Used by permission. All rights reserved.

Scripture quotations marked TLB are taken from *The Living Bible*, copyright © 1971 by Tyndale House Publishers, Wheaton, Ill. Used by permission.

Scripture quotations marked NIV are taken from *The Holy Bible, New International Version*. Copyright © 1973, 1978, 1984, International Bible Society. Used by permission of Zondervan Bible Publishers.

Parent page artwork copyright © 2005 Diane Bay.

Paul Loth, *My First Study Bible* (Nashville, Tenn.: Thomas Nelson, 1994).

Page design by Educational Publishing Concepts, Inc., P.O. Box 665, Wheaton, IL 60189.

ISBN 1-4185-0626-5

Printed in the United States of America.
06 07 08 09 10 VG 9 8 7 6 5 4 3 2 1

Introduction

The ABC's of the Bible is a culmination of my dream to make the Bible come alive for young children. As an early-childhood educator, I believe that God has given preschool-age children special gifts to help them know Him in an intimate way. In fact, Jesus even made that clear in Mark 10:14, saying:

"Let the little children come to me. Don't stop them. The kingdom of God belongs to people who are like these little children" (ICB).

Young children learn best through repetition, routines, movement, and predictability. So *The ABC's of the Bible* is based on a familiar routine, consisting of a story, discussion, craft, weekly Bible verse, snack, worship, and prayer. For use in a weekly church setting, we have provided a parent page and coloring-book page for each lesson that can be sent home with each child. These pages will communicate to the parents the theme of the week that the child has been studying, the weekly Bible verse, and suggested ways to reinforce the lesson at home.

The ABC's of the Bible is intended to foster an interactive learning experience for children—whether the study is done at home or in a classroom setting. At the beginning of each lesson, we will introduce a Bible character using the narrative found in *My First Study Bible*, a wonderful Bible resource for children. As you lead the children through this fifty-two-week curriculum, the children will meet a new Bible character each week, leading them through the stories in the Bible and making the messages come alive for their young hearts.

This curriculum is perfect for at-home use with your children and is an ideal curriculum for small and large churches alike—full of ideas, activities, take-home pages, and crafts available on an enclosed CD-ROM for easy duplication.

We are so excited that you have chosen *The ABC's of the Bible* to make the Bible come alive for the children in your life. Be creative and have fun!

—Lisa Woodruff, Little Kids Worship

Contents

Adam and the Apple
Lesson Theme: God always forgives.

Materials:

- Apple wedges for snack
- Red, green, and yellow paint
- Construction paper
- Red, green, and yellow apples
- Paintbrushes
- Knife to cut apple

Bible Character: Adam

Bible Verse

"He has taken our sins away from us as far as the east is from west." Psalm 103:12 ICB

Bible Story

My First Study Bible pp. 14–20, "God Gave Us a Beautiful Home"

Story Application:

- God told Adam and Eve not to eat from the special tree. Adam and Eve disobeyed God and ate from the special tree. Did God still love Adam and Eve even after they ate from the tree? (Yes.) Then why did God have to punish them? (Adam and Eve disobeyed God. Since they did not obey, they could not live near the special tree anymore.)
- Sometimes when we do things that are wrong, our moms and dads have to punish us, too. Do you think they still love us? (Reassure the children that God and their parents always love them. It is because of this love that they discipline them.)
- God loves us all the time, even when we disobey. You know that Adam and Eve ate the apple, but do you know that God put a surprise in the apple for us? (Cut the apple in half, dividing the top from the bottom, and you will find...) A STAR!
- God promises to always forgive us when we do something wrong and are truly sorry. God can turn something sad into a beautiful star, just like He did with the apple.

Snack

Apple wedges

Craft

Using the cut apples from the story, paint the apple halves with red, green, or yellow paint. Then use the apples as stamps to make star prints on construction paper.

Closing Prayer

Dear God, please forgive me when I sin. Use my life to make something beautiful.

1

Parent Page

Aa Adam and the Apple

Dear Parent,

Today your child heard the story of Adam and Eve—how they disobeyed God and ate from the Tree of Life. From this lesson, we learned how God loves us even when we sin. There is a special surprise hidden in an apple when you cut the apple, dividing the top of the apple from the bottom. (It's a star!) When we ask God to forgive our sins, our lives can be like the beautiful stars we find in apples.

This week try these fun activities with your child:

(1) Make homemade applesauce: Peel and cut 6 apples into chunks. Put a few chunks of apples and 3/4 cup of water into a blender. Blend. Continue to add the apples until all are blended and soft. Add sugar and cinnamon to taste.

(2) Plant apple seeds in a cup and water every few days. Plant your apple tree outside next spring!

(3) Learn Today's Verse: "He has taken our sins away from us as far as the east is from west." Psalm 103:12 ICB

Adam and the Apple

"He has taken our sins away from us
as far as the east is from west."
Psalm 103:12 ICB

Noah's Ark
Lesson Theme: God keeps His promises.

Materials:

- Cool Whip
- Small plates and spoons
- Round rainbow cereal
- Animal stickers (2 for each animal)
- Parachute or large golf umbrella
- Cotton balls
- Rainbow craft page
- Crayons
- Glue

Bible Character: Noah

Bible Verse

"I have placed my rainbow in the clouds as a sign of my promise." Genesis 9:13 TLB

Bible Story

My First Study Bible pp. 21–26, "God Kept Me Safe"

Story Application:

- Teacher, hold a parachute (or umbrella) up over the story carpet for this activity. Give each child 2 animal stickers. The teacher will be God, and the children, little Noahs. God will tell the little Noahs to bring 2 of each animal into the ark. Then, once all the children are in the ark (under the parachute or umbrella), pretend to make rain.
- After the rain, have the children come out of the "ark" and thank God for taking away the rain.

Snack

Give each child a small plate with a spoonful of Cool Whip. Add about 10 colored rainbow cereal pieces to the cloud. Repeat the Bible verse: "I have placed my rainbow in the clouds as a sign of my promise" (Genesis 9:13 TLB).

Craft

Have children color the rainbow on the craft page and glue cotton balls to the clouds.

Closing Prayer

Dear God, thank You for keeping Your promises to me. Please help me to keep my promises to others.

Parent Page

Aa Noah's Ark

Dear Parent,

Today your child heard the story of Noah and the big Flood. We learned

that God promised never to send a flood that would cover the whole earth again. We

learned that we can trust God to keep His promises.

This week try these fun activities with your child:

Use a watering hose and stand with your back to the sun. When you spray the water, a beautiful rainbow will appear.

Visit the zoo and talk about all the beautiful animals God created.

Learn Today's Verse:
"I have placed my rainbow in the clouds as a sign of my promise."
Genesis 9:13 TLB

Noah's Ark

"I have placed my rainbow in the
clouds as a sign of my promise."
Genesis 9:13 TLB

# Blessings to Hannah
Lesson Theme: Blessings are answered prayers.

 ## Materials:
• Paper and crayons

 ## Bible Character: Hannah

 ## Bible Verse
"Hannah said: 'The Lord has filled my heart with joy . . . I am glad because you have helped me!'" 1 Samuel 2:1 ICB

 ## Bible Story
My First Study Bible, pp. 122–26, "My Prayer Was Answered"
Story Application:
- Anytime we talk to God, we are praying. Sometimes we tell God about our day. Like Adam and Eve, we can pray to God and ask Him to forgive our sins. Other times when we pray to God, we can ask Him to bless us.
- Let's make a list of blessings we ask God for. (good health, good weather, friends)
- Hannah prayed for a baby for a long time. God hears us, but sometimes we need to wait to have our prayers answered. Why do you think we would need to wait? We need to be patient for God's answers to our prayers.

 ## Craft
Have children draw a picture on a piece of paper of something they are praying for. Pray with children individually as you walk around and talk with them about their drawings.

 ## Closing Prayer
Dear God, thank You for all the blessings You have given to me.

Parent Page

Bb Blessings to Hannah

Dear Parent,

Today your child heard the story about Hannah and how she wanted to have a baby. Hannah prayed for a baby, and God answered her prayer. We learned to be patient and wait for God to answer our prayers. We also learned that when God answers "yes," it is a blessing.

This week try these fun activities with your child:

① Pray with your child each night before bed. Specifically ask what he or she wants to pray for.

② Share with your child a time when you prayed and God answered your prayer.

③ Learn Today's Verse:
"Hannah said: 'The Lord has filled my heart with joy . . . I am glad because you have helped me!'"
1 Samuel 2:1 ICB

Blessings to Hannah

"Hannah said: 'The Lord has filled my heart with joy . . . I am glad because you have helped me!'"
1 Samuel 2:1 ICB

The Boy King

Lesson Theme: We will obey God.

Materials:
- Josiah craft page
- Yellow, red, and brown crayons for each child

Bible Character: Josiah

Bible Verse

"There was no king like Josiah . . . He obeyed the Lord with all his heart, soul and strength."
2 Kings 23:25 ICB

Bible Story

My First Study Bible pp. 197–206, "I Obeyed God"

Story Application:
- When Josiah was fixing the temple, he found the scrolls of God's Word. Josiah had never seen these before. Can you imagine if you had never seen a Bible before?
- When Josiah read the scrolls and learned about God's laws, he realized he had been disobeying God. Josiah read the Bible just as we do to learn how to obey God and about God's love for us.
- Today we are going to play "Teacher Says." Listen closely to hear what I am saying and follow my directions.

Teacher-Says Game (similar to "Simon Says"):
Teacher, give the children directions, but they should obey only if you say, "Teacher says." For example, "Teacher says, touch your feet. (Obey.) Teacher says, wiggle your hands. (Obey.) Touch your nose. (Do not obey—Teacher didn't say!)" Have fun playing this game.

Craft

We are so blessed to have Bibles to read! It is important for us to learn to obey God, our parents, and teachers in authority over us. Today we are going to color our papers in a special way. Listen closely and obey the teacher!

Teacher, give the children these directions:
1. Color Josiah's crown yellow. 2. Color the book brown. 3. Color the heart red.

Closing Prayer

Dear God, thank You for the gift of Your Word. Help me to obey.

Parent Page
Bb The Boy King

Dear Parent,

Today we heard the story about Josiah, who was only eight when he

became king! We learned how blessed we are to have the Bible to read and to help us

learn to obey God.

This week try these fun activities with your child:

(1)

Play "Mom Says" or "Dad Says." Give your child directions, but he or she should obey only if you say, "Mom [or Dad] says." For example, "Mom says, touch your feet. (Obey.) Dad says, wiggle your hands. (Obey.) Touch your nose. (Do not obey—Mom [or Dad] didn't say!)"

(2)

Thank your child as he or she obeys you this week. Catch your child being good!

(3)

Learn Today's Verse:

"There was no king like

Josiah . . . He obeyed the

Lord with all his heart,

soul and strength."

2 Kings 23:25 ICB

The Boy King

"There was no king like Josiah . . . He obeyed the Lord with all his heart, soul and strength."
2 Kings 23:25 ICB

The Children Jesus Loves

Lesson Theme: Jesus loves children.

Materials:

- Magazine pictures of children
- Large paper heart
- Sticker hearts (1 for each child)
- Paper people
- Wiggly eyes, yarn, and paper to glue on
- Glue

Bible Character: Peter

Bible Verse

"Jesus . . . said to them, 'Let the little children come to me. Don't stop them. The kingdom of God belongs to people who are like these little children.'" Mark 10:14 ICB

Bible Story

My First Study Bible, pp. 384–88, "Jesus Loves Children"

Story Application:

- Show pictures of different children. How are they different? How are they alike? Jesus loves ALL the children. How can we love each other? Our friends?
- Hold up the large heart with a sheet of stickers hidden facing you. Give each child a sticker heart to wear from Jesus' "big heart." Jesus' heart is big enough to love everyone!
- Sing "Jesus Loves the Little Children."

Song: Jesus loves the little children,
All the children of the world.
Red and yellow, black and white,
They are precious in His sight.
Jesus loves the little children of the world.

Craft

Have children create paper people. Decorate with yarn for hair, wiggly eyes, and paper for clothing. After all the paper children are put together, reenact the story of the children coming to Jesus.

Closing Prayer

Dear God, thank You for loving me. (Go around the circle and thank God for each child by name.)

Parent Page

Cc The Children Jesus Loves

Dear Parent,

Today your child heard the story of Jesus calling the little children to Him and blessing them. We learned that Jesus loves all the children of the world.

This week try these fun activities with your child:

 1

Look through family pictures. Make sure to show pictures of yourself as a child.

 2

Take an afternoon and be a kid again! Go to the park with your child. Swing on the swings, and go down the slide.

 3

Learn Today's Verse: "Jesus . . . said to them, 'Let the little children come to me. Don't stop them. The kingdom of God belongs to people who are like these little children.'"

Mark 10:14 ICB

The Children Jesus Loves

"Jesus . . . said to them, 'Let the little children come to me. Don't stop them. The kingdom of God belongs to people who are like these little children.'"

Mark 10:14 ICB

The Coat of Many Colors

Lesson Theme: We are all special.

Materials:

- Coffee filters
- Spray bottle filled with water
- Washable bold-tip markers
- Paper towels

Bible Character: Joseph

Bible Verse

"I praise you because you made me in an amazing and wonderful way."
Psalm 139:14 ICB

Bible Story

My First Study Bible pp. 34–39, "God Makes Good from Bad"

Story Application:

- Joseph's dad made him a special colorful coat. Joseph's brothers were jealous and did mean things to Joseph because they did not have special rainbow-colored coats.
- Life is not always fair, and everything is not always even. However, as much as possible, we need to think about other people's feelings and include others. Joseph was a very special boy, and Joseph's dad made him a special coat. God has made each of us with special gifts.
- Today we are going to make rainbow filters for your family, friends, and neighbors. Give them away with a smile, and let the people around you know how special you think they are.

Craft

Using markers, make designs and squiggles on the coffee filters, covering them with ink. When they are done, lay each coffee filter one at a time on 2 paper towels. Squirt the coffee filters with water, and watch the colors blend together. Hang the coffee filters to dry, placing paper towels under them in case they drip. When you are finished, share your rainbows with others and brighten their day!

Closing Prayer

Dear God, thank You for making me special.

Parent Page

Cc The Coat of Many Colors

Dear Parent,

Today your child heard the story of Joseph and his rainbow-colored coat. We learned that God made us all with special gifts and talents. We want to share those gifts with those around us.

This week try these fun activities with your child:

① Deliver the rainbow filters your child made to your neighbors' houses, and spend some time getting to know your neighbors better.

② One night at bedtime, share with your child the special gifts you see in him or her.

③ Learn Today's Verse:
"I praise you because you made me in an amazing and wonderful way."
Psalm 139:14 ICB

The Coat of Many Colors

"I praise you because you made me
in an amazing and wonderful way."
Psalm 139:14 ICB

Dd David and Goliath
Lesson Theme: God is a living God.

Materials:
- Tin foil cut for each child
- Construction paper
- Glue sticks

Bible Character: David

Bible Verse
"David said to him . . . 'I come to you in the name of the Lord of heaven's armies. He's the God of the armies of Israel!'"
1 Samuel 17:45 ICB

Bible Story
My First Study Bible, pp. 141–49, "I Was a Giant Killer"
Story Application:
- Goliath was a LOT bigger than David was, but David knew that his God was a LOT bigger than Goliath. David knew God would protect him. Do you believe God is strong and powerful? Stronger than any man?
- David did not use Saul's armor, because it was too big for him. He used a few rocks and a sling. That is what David had always used to keep his sheep safe from lions and bears. You don't need to have special things or clothes for God to use you. He can use you just as you are.
- What can you do to help God? (Love people, help people, be kind . . .)

Craft
Have each child glue a piece of tin foil onto a piece of construction paper, using glue sticks. Have the children look into the tin foil and "see" themselves. Remind them that they are important to God, and God will help them when they need Him. Their God is the God of the armies of Israel!

Closing Prayer
Dear God, thank You for making me just the way You made me. Please use me in Your plans on the earth.

Parent Page

Dd David and Goliath

Dear Parent,

Today your child heard the story of David and Goliath. Our God is powerful!

We learned that we do not need to have special things for God to use us. God will use us

with the talents we already have.

This week try these fun activities with your child:

 1

Show your child how God is ALIVE! God's creation is all around us—in a rainbow, a newborn baby, animals, flowers, trees, and so on.

 3

Learn Today's Verse: "David said to him . . . 'I come to you in the name of the Lord of heaven's armies. He's the God of the armies of Israel!'" 1 Samuel 17:45 ICB

2

Think out loud with your child about what God would do in the situations you face every day.

David and Goliath

"David said to him . . . 'I come to you in the name of the Lord of heaven's armies. He's the God of the armies of Israel!'"
1 Samuel 17:45 ICB

Dd Daniel and the Lions' Den
Lesson Theme: God will protect us.

Materials:

- Animal crackers for snack
- Animal crackers for craft
- Construction paper
- Glue

Bible Character: Daniel

Bible Verse

"Daniel's God is the living God . . . God rescues and saves people. God does mighty miracles in heaven and on earth." Daniel 6:26–27 ICB

Bible Story

My First Study Bible, pp. 279–85, "A Strange Place to Spend the Night"
Story Application:

- The people wanted Daniel to pray to the king, but Daniel knew he should pray only to God. Daniel did what was right, even though everyone around him did not. God protected Daniel from the lions in the den.

Snack

Animal crackers

Craft

Have children draw Daniel on their paper. Glue the animal crackers on the construction paper with Daniel. Talk about how God saved Daniel because Daniel trusted God more than he trusted the king. Repeat the Bible verse.

Closing Prayer

Dear God, thank You for being so powerful. Please keep me safe.

Parent Page

Dd Daniel and the Lions' Den

Dear Parent,

Today your child heard the story about Daniel and the lions' den. We learned God will protect us when we follow Him.

This week try these fun activities with your child:

(1)

This week, try to be more aware of God's protection in your everyday life. Point out what you notice to your child. Say a short prayer of thanks to God for His protection.

(2)

Watch the Veggie Tales video, *Where's God When I'm Scared?* with your child. Talk about how to rely on God in scary situations.

(3)

Learn Today's Verse: "Daniel's God is the living God . . . God rescues and saves people. God does mighty miracles in heaven and on earth."

Daniel 6:26–27 ICB

Daniel and the Lions' Den

"Daniel's God is the living God . . . God rescues and saves people. God does mighty miracles in heaven and on earth."
Daniel 6:26–27 ICB

Elijah
Lesson Theme: God provides.

Materials:
- A slice of bread for each child
- 2 cups oil
- 12 cups flour
- 2 cups water
- Large bowl and wooden spoon
- Plastic zipper bags

Bible Character: Elijah

Bible Verse
"The birds brought Elijah bread and meat every morning and every evening."
1 Kings 17:6 ICB

Bible Story
My First Study Bible, pp. 167–72, "God Takes Care of Me"
Story Application:
- Elijah was a special person called a prophet. A prophet can hear God talking to him. Prophets tell people what God tells them. Today we hear God's voice in our hearts and through the Bible.
- Just as God provided protection for Daniel in the lions' den, God provided food for Elijah. God used birds each day to carry bread and meat to Elijah.

Snack
Bread (brought by ravens). Teachers, fly around the room and pretend to be ravens bringing each of the children a slice of bread.

Craft
Bread is made by mixing dough and cooking it. We are going to make play dough today. After we mix it, we can play with it instead of baking it. But remember—we can't eat it!

Teacher, mix 2 cups oil, 2 cups water, and 12 cups of flour to make play dough with class. Divide out homemade play dough for the children to play with. Let the children take home their play dough in plastic zipper bags.

Closing Prayer
Dear God, thank You for providing food for my family.

Parent Page
Ee Elijah

Dear Parent,

Today your child heard the story about how God used birds to carry food to

Elijah. We learned that God provides for His prophets.

This week try these fun activities with your child:

①

Make bread from scratch. How long does it take to bake? How much flour did you use?

②

Talk to your child about how God provides food for your family.

③

Take food to a local food bank with your child. Talk to your child about how God provides for others through us.

④

Learn Today's Verse: "The birds brought Elijah bread and meat every morning and every evening." 1 Kings 17:6 ICB

Elijah

"The birds brought Elijah bread and meat every morning and every evening."
1 Kings 17:6 ICB

E e The Egyptian Plagues

Lesson Theme: God is powerful.

Materials:
- Bowl
- Whole milk
- Food coloring
- Dish soap

Bible Character: Moses

Bible Verse

"The angel of the Lord appeared to Moses in flames of fire coming
out of a bush. Moses saw that the bush was on fire, but it was not burning up."
Exodus 3:2 ICB

Bible Story

My First Study Bible, pp.48–56, "God Teaches Pharaoh a Lesson"
Story Application:
- God is so powerful! God made the bush burn without hurting the bush. God made the stick become a snake. God made the water turn to blood.
- Moses warned Pharaoh about each plague before it came. It is hard for us to see why Pharaoh wouldn't listen to Moses and turn to God. But Pharaoh was not focusing on God.
- Pharaoh was watching the magicians. When they were able to do things like the plagues of God, Pharaoh followed them. As the plagues continued, the magicians were not able to do what only the power of God could do.

Craft

Teacher, fill a bowl half full of whole milk. Next, drop ten drops of food coloring in the milk. Let the colors swirl around, and then drop one drop of dish soap in the milk.

What happened to the colors? Are they all gone, or did they just move? When we sin, only God has the power to cleanse and take away sin through the blood of Jesus. Our actions may remove the evidence, but not the sin. Keep your eyes on God and His plans for your life, and be on the lookout for the "magicians" around you.

(Note: To redo the experiment, start with a fresh bowl of milk.)

Closing Prayer

Dear God, thank You for taking away my sins through the blood of Jesus.

Parent Page

Ee The Egyptian Plagues

Dear Parent,

Today your child heard the story of God talking to Moses in the burning bush, and the story of the Egyptian plagues. We learned to keep our eyes on God and His plans for our lives, and not to be tricked by the "magicians" around us who pretend to be gods.

This week try these fun activities with your child:

1

If you know how to do "magic," show your child a trick. Then explain how you performed your trick. Tell your child that we must always look to God and not what our eyes see to know what is good and true.

2

Help your child visualize the burning bush by lighting a branch on fire and watching it burn. Explain that when God appeared as fire to Moses, the branches were on fire, but they did not burn up.

3

Learn Today's Verse: "The angel of the Lord appeared to Moses in flames of fire coming out of a bush. Moses saw that the bush was on fire, but it was not burning up." Exodus 3:2 ICB

The Egyptian Plagues

"The angel of the Lord appeared to Moses in flames of fire coming out of a bush. Moses saw that the bush was on fire, but it was not burning up."

Exodus 3:2 ICB

Ff Faith in the Fiery Furnace

Lesson Theme: Put your faith in God.

Materials:
- Tissue-paper squares cut out of red, orange, and yellow tissue paper
- Glue sticks
- Fire craft page
- Blindfold

Bible Character: Daniel

Bible Verse

"You can throw us into the blazing furnace. The God we serve is able to save us."
Daniel 3:17 ICB

Bible Story

My First Study Bible, pp. 272–78, "Shadrach, Meshach, and Abednego"

Story Application:
- Just as Daniel did, Shadrach, Meshach, and Abednego would only pray to God. God protected them just as He protected Daniel in the lions' den.
- When they were in the fiery furnace, there was another person there with them. Who do you think it was? (an angel, Jesus)
- That angel was sent by God to protect Shadrach, Meshach, and Abednego. God sent the angel because they had faith and believed that God would protect them. Do you have faith that God will protect you?
- Demonstrate putting faith in someone by blindfolding one teacher and having another teacher lead him or her around the room. Just as the teacher with the blindfold can't see who is leading him or her, we can't see God when He leads us. We have to have faith that He is there guiding us. Faith is trusting and believing even when we can't see.

Craft

Give each child a craft page. Have the children glue orange, red, and yellow tissue squares onto the pattern of the flames.

Closing Prayer

Dear God, thank You for protecting us.

Parent Page

Ff Faith in the Fiery Furnace

Dear Parent,

Today your child heard the story of Shadrach, Meshach, and Abednego in

the fiery furnace. We learned that faith is trusting and believing God even when we can't

see what He is going to do.

This week try these fun activities with your child:

1
Talk to your child about the ways you are leading him or her, and the ways others lead you.

2
Watch the Veggie Tales movie *Rack, Shack, and Benny.*

3
Blindfold each family member, one at a time, and lead each other around your house as you talk about faith.

4
Learn Today's Verse: "You can throw us into the blazing furnace. The God we serve is able to save us." Daniel 3:17 ICB

Faith in the Fiery Furnace

"You can throw us into the blazing
furnace. The God we serve is able to
save us."
Daniel 3:17 ICB

Ff Freedom from Chains

Lesson Theme: Prayer is powerful.

Materials:

- 80# copy paper (or a heavy-weight paper) cut into 1-inch strips (2 for each child)
- Crepe paper
- Stapler
- Choir robe for teacher
- Tape

Bible Character: Peter

Bible Verse

"Peter was kept in jail. But the church kept on praying to God for him."
Acts 12:5 ICB

Bible Story

My First Study Bible, pp. 461–68, "The Angel Helps Me"

Story Application:

- Peter was put in jail because he told people the "Good News" about Jesus. Peter's friends prayed for his safety.
- An angel rescued Peter from the prison. Both of Peter's hands were handcuffed to a guard. Only God could set Peter free. Stop here and make the craft.
- Have the children come back to the group and sit in a semicircle. Role-play the story, with each child having a turn to be set free. Teacher, put on the choir robe and be the angel.
- Have the first child come to the front. Lead the children in praying for that child to be set free. When the children pray, the "angel" appears. The child then breaks his or her crepe-paper chains and is led by the angel out of the circle.
- Repeat for all children.

Craft

We are going to make handcuffs like Peter's. First, staple 80# strips around each child's wrists. Next, tape crepe paper to the "handcuffs," connecting them together. Have the children carefully sit in a semicircle with their handcuffs on.

Closing Prayer

Dear God, thank You that You hear my prayers!

Parent Page

Ff Freedom from Chains

Dear Parent,

Today your child heard the story about when God freed Peter from jail. We learned that Peter's friends were praying for his release and that God sent an angel to free him.

This week try these fun activities with your child:

1

Pray with your child that God will keep your family safe. Teach your child to trust God daily for his or her safety.

2

When you and your child see an ambulance on the way to the hospital, say a quick prayer for that person's safety.

3

Learn Today's Verse: "Peter was kept in jail. But the church kept on praying to God for him." Acts 12:5 ICB

Freedom from Chains

"Peter was kept in jail. But the church kept on praying to God for him."
Acts 12:5 ICB

Gg Grace Given to Peter
Lesson Theme: Jesus offers us grace.

Materials:

- Sugar cookies with sprinkles for snack
- Empty toilet-paper rolls
- 2 4-inch squares of clear cellophane or wax paper for each child
- 2 cups rice mixed with glitter
- White construction paper cut to 3 x 4 inches to go around toilet-paper roll
- Tape

Bible Character: Peter

Bible Verse

"You are a kind and merciful God." Nehemiah 9:31 ICB

Bible Story

My First Study Bible, pp. 334–40, "I Denied Knowing My Best Friend"

Story Application:

- Peter said he did not know Jesus even though he did. When Jesus saw Peter, was He upset with him? NO! He reminded Peter to try again and tell everyone about Him.
- Jesus loves us. When we ask Him to forgive us because we've done something wrong, He gives us His grace. Grace allows us to start over and try again to do what Jesus asks of us. Grace is something Jesus gives us that we don't deserve and that we cannot earn. It is a very special gift.
- Today we are going to have a very special snack. (Pass out cookies.) These are yummy cookies. Do you see the special sprinkles on top? Grace is like the sprinkles on your cookies. It is sweet and special. Grace makes everything better.

Snack

Grace cookies (cookies with sprinkles)

Craft

We are going to make a pretend tube of "glitter grace." Jesus "sprinkles" grace down from heaven to us. Our "glitter grace" reminds us of our need for Jesus' real grace.

Tape clear cellophane (or wax paper) to one end of the tube, adhering four corners of cellophane with tape. Then use tape to seal cellophane around tube. Add rice glitter, and tape clear cellophane to the other end. Have children decorate one side of precut construction paper. When they are finished, tape their paper around the tube.

Closing Prayer

Dear God, thank You for Your grace to me.

Parent Page
Gg Grace Given to Peter

Dear Parent,

Today your child heard the story about Jesus forgiving Peter for denying

Him. We learned about grace. Grace allows us to start over and try again to do what

Jesus asks of us. Grace is something Jesus gives us that we don't deserve and that we

cannot earn. It is a very special gift.

This week try these fun activities with your child:

① Watch the Veggie Tales movie *God Wants Me to Forgive Them?* Then discuss what forgiveness means.

③ Learn Today's Verse: "You are a kind and merciful God." Nehemiah 9:31 ICB

② Talk with your child about the importance of asking for forgiveness when he or she has done something wrong. Remind yourself that you may sometimes need to ask your child for forgiveness too.

Grace Given to Peter

"You are a kind and merciful God."
Nehemiah 9:31 ICB

Gideon

Lesson Theme: God speaks to us.

Materials:

- Construction paper cut to bookmark size
- A piece of fleece
- Stickers, crayons, and markers to decorate bookmarks

Bible Character: Gideon

Bible Verse

"All Scripture is given by God and is useful for teaching and for showing people what is wrong in their lives." 2 Timothy 3:16 ICB

Bible Story

My First Study Bible, pp. 100–105, "God Speaks to Me"

Story Application:

- How did God show Gideon He was talking to him? (by answering his requests)
- How does God show us He is talking to us? (through the Bible, church)
- Show children a piece of fleece. Explain how Gideon used the fleece to hear from God.
- God still speaks to us today. God speaks through people and the Bible. We can trust the Bible to show us what God wants us to do.

Craft

Today we are going to decorate Bible bookmarks. Encourage the children to take their bookmarks home and put them in their Bibles.

Closing Prayer

Dear God, thank You for giving me the Bible to guide me.

Parent Page
Gg Gideon

Dear Parent,

Today your child heard the story of how God talked to Gideon. We made

Bible bookmarks to keep our places as we read from the Bible and learn about God's

Word.

This week try these fun activities with your child:

1

Read a Bible story together. Have your child use his or her bookmark to mark where you are in the Bible.

2

Encourage your child to read a Bible story each night before going to bed.

3

Learn Today's Verse: "All Scripture is given by God and is useful for teaching and for showing people what is wrong in their lives." 2 Timothy 3:16 ICB

Gideon

"All Scripture is given by God and is useful for teaching and for showing people what is wrong in their lives."
2 Timothy 3:16 ICB

Healing the Paralyzed Man
Lesson Theme: Jesus heals.

Materials:
- Get-well cards copied on colorful copy paper
- Stickers, crayons, and markers to decorate cards
- Lunch bags to store cards (1 for each child)

Bible Character: Paralyzed Man

Bible Verse

"Jesus went everywhere in Galilee . . . And he healed all the people's diseases and sicknesses."
Matthew 4:23 ICB

Bible Story

My First Study Bible, pp. 342–46, "Jesus Healed Me"
Story Application:
- God has the power to heal people. Jesus is God's Son. He also has the power to heal people. Today doctors and nurses are also used by God to heal people.
- Do you know how you can help heal people? You can pray to God for their healing, you can make them cards, and you can keep them company.

Craft

Have children decorate get-well cards using crayons, markers, and stickers. The children may use the cards for friends they know are sick, and keep some for later. Give each child a lunch bag in which to store cards.

Closing Prayer

Dear God, thank You for Your healing power.

I am praying that
Jesus will make
you well.

Love,

Get
Well
Soon

Parent Page

Hh Healing the Paralyzed Man

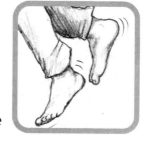

Dear Parent,

Today your child heard the story of the paralyzed man who was healed. We learned that we can help sick people by praying for them, making them cards, and keeping them company.

This week try these fun activities with your child:

① Encourage your child to pray for people who are sick and hurting.

② Send your child's get-well cards to sick friends who could use some cheering up.

③ Learn Today's Verse: "Jesus went everywhere in Galilee . . . And he healed all the people's diseases and sicknesses." Matthew 4:23 ICB

Healing the Paralyzed Man

"Jesus went everywhere in Galilee . . .
And he healed all the people's
diseases and sicknesses."
Matthew 4:23 ICB

The Holy Spirit Sent to the Disciples
Lesson Theme: The Holy Spirit guides us.

Materials:
- Holy Spirit craft page
- Red, yellow, and orange paint
- Paintbrushes
- Gold glitter

Bible Character: Peter

Bible Verse

"God has poured out his love to fill our hearts. God gave us his love through the Holy Spirit." Romans 5:5 ICB

Bible Story

My First Study Bible, pp. 441–47, "I Tell People About Jesus"
Story Application:
- God gave a special gift to His disciples: the gift of the Holy Spirit. How did the gift come? What did it look like? (wind and fire)
- When we ask Jesus to forgive our sins and we accept Him as our Lord and Savior, He gives us the gift of the Holy Spirit. The Holy Spirit helps us to understand God's will and follow Him. Did you notice the people could understand one another after the Holy Spirit came?
- The Holy Spirit is a very special gift from God.

Craft

Paint the Holy Spirit fire on the craft page. While the picture is still wet, sprinkle a little gold glitter on the fire to make it shimmer.

Closing Prayer

Dear God, thank You for sending the Holy Spirit to guide me.

Parent Page

Hh The Holy Spirit Sent to the Disciples

Dear Parent,

Today your child heard the story about how God sent the Holy Spirit to the disciples. Your child learned about the Holy Spirit and His ability to guide us. What other people guide your child? Focus this week on sharing with your child when and how he or she is guided.

This week try these fun activities with your child:

1 Focus this week on sharing with your child how he or she is guided by you to make good decisions.

2 Watch TV commercials with your child on Saturday morning and talk with your child about how the people who sell those products are "guiding" children to want their toys, food, etc.

3 Learn Today's Verse: "God has poured out his love to fill our hearts. God gave us his love through the Holy Spirit." Romans 5:5 ICB

The Holy Spirit Sent to the Disciples

"God has poured out his love to fill
our hearts. God gave us his love
through the Holy Spirit."
Romans 5:5 ICB

I Worship Jesus

Lesson Theme: We worship God.

Materials:

- Worship God craft page
- Crayons and markers

Bible Character: Elijah

Bible Verse

"If the Lord is the true God, follow him." 1 Kings 18:21 ICB

Bible Story

My First Study Bible, pp.173–81, "God Is Up to the Challenge"

Story Application:

- How did Elijah prove that God was more powerful than their stone Baal gods? (God burned up the sacrifice of Elijah.)
- Why did Elijah pour water on the wood before he prayed for God to "burn it up"? (So that it would be harder to burn)
- Elijah proved that God was the One deserving of worship and praise. How do we worship God? (by singing, praying, and saying good things about God)
- Today we are going to worship God by singing our favorite songs. (Sing praise songs from your church together.)
- We can also worship God through prayer. Have children suggest things to pray for and lead them in group prayer. Allow children to pray out loud, as well.

Craft

Worship God craft page. Have the children color the different ways to worship God, and draw any additional ways they think of.

Closing Prayer

Dear God, thank You for allowing me to worship You.

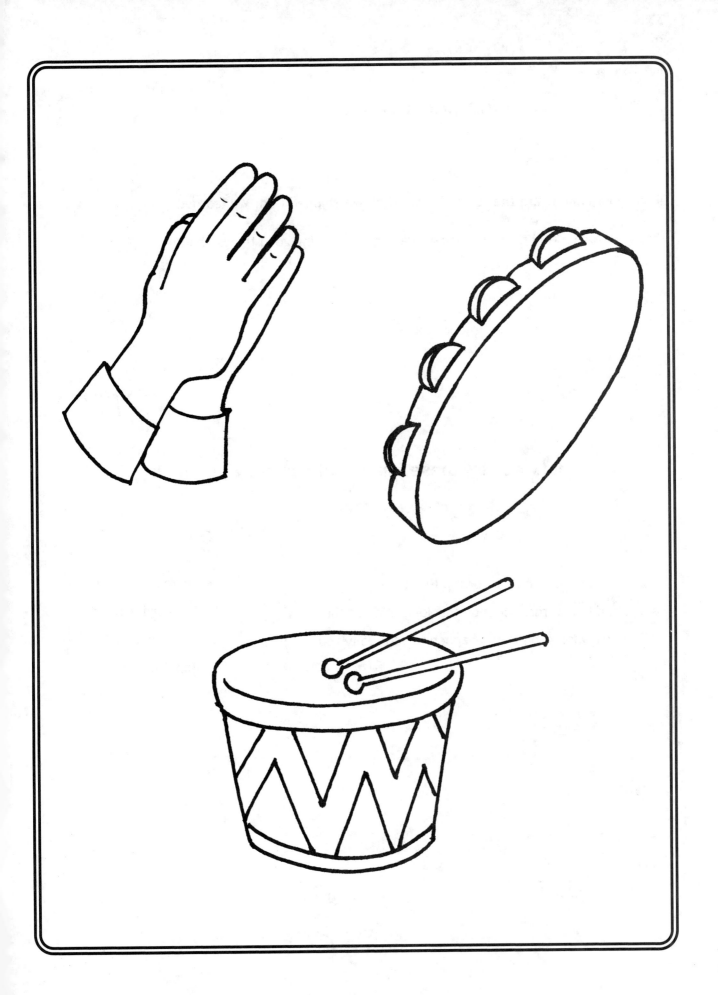

Parent Page

Ii I Worship Jesus

Dear Parent,

Today your child heard the story of how Elijah worshipped God. We learned

that we worship God through singing, praying, and saying good things about God.

This week try these fun activities with your child:

① Today we learned how to worship God through prayer, song, and our words. Focus on thanking God out loud this week when good things happen in your daily routine.

③ Learn Today's Verse:
"If the Lord is the true God, follow him."
1 Kings 18:21 ICB

② Listen to Christian music in the car and worship God as you go about your errands.

I Worship Jesus

"If the Lord is the true God, follow him."
1 Kings 18:21 ICB

Jj Joshua in Jericho
Lesson Theme: Joshua was faithful.

Materials:
- Sugar cubes
- Small paper plates
- Glue (not glue sticks)
- Large building blocks or shoeboxes

Bible Character: Joshua

Bible Verse
"Then Joshua gave the command: 'Now, shout! The Lord has given you this city!'"
Joshua 6:16 ICB

Bible Story
My First Study Bible, pp.93–98, "God Knocked Down the Walls of Jericho"
Story Application:
- God told Joshua to march around the city for seven days. It sounds pretty silly to think that marching around a city will make the walls fall down, doesn't it?
- God wasn't asking Joshua to make the walls fall down. He was asking Joshua to obey Him, and God made the walls fall down.
- Sometimes we don't know why our parents or God asks us to do things, but we should obey them and do what we are told.
- Build a wall out of the large blocks. Have the children march around the wall of blocks seven times. When they are finished, give a large shout together, and the teacher then gently knocks the wall down.

Craft
Using sugar cubes and glue, have the children build a wall on the paper plates to remind them of God's power when they are faithful.

Closing Prayer
Dear God, I will be faithful and obey You.

Parent Page

Jj Joshua in Jericho

Dear Parent,

Today your child heard the story of Joshua and the battle of Jericho. We

learned that God was not asking Joshua to knock down the walls of Jericho. God was ask-

ing Joshua to obey Him, and God made the walls fall down.

This week try these fun activities with your child:

(1)

Watch the Veggie Tales movie *Josh and the Big Wall* as a family.

(2)

Point out to your child the times when he or she is faithful and obeys you without question this week.

(3)

Learn Today's Verse: "Then Joshua gave the command: 'Now, shout! The Lord has given you this city!'" Joshua 6:16 ICB

Joshua in Jericho

"Then Joshua gave the command:
'Now, shout! The Lord has
given you this city!'"
Joshua 6:16 ICB

Jj Job

Lesson Theme: Job trusted God.

Materials:

- Crayons
- Job craft page

Bible Character: Job

Bible Verse

"[Job] said: '. . . The Lord gave these things to me. And he has taken them away. Praise the name of the Lord.'"

Job 1:21 ICB

Bible Story

My First Study Bible, pp. 245–51, "I'm Glad I Didn't Give Up on God"

Story Application:

- Job trusted God to take care of him. Even when Job lost all he had, he still loved God and trusted God to take care of him.
- What is your favorite toy? Do you love God more than that toy? If you lost your toy, would you still love God? That was how Job felt. He was sad he lost everything, but that did not change his love for God.
- God loves you even more than you love Him! Even though we can't see God, we must trust Him and love Him more than the things we can see.

Craft

Have the children name items that are important to them that they "love." (dolls, trucks, toys, etc.) Then read the activity sheet to them: "Jesus, I love You more than my favorite _____. Thank You for all my blessings." Have the children pick one item to draw on the page, and write the name of the item in the blank. When they are finished, go around the table and have children share what they drew.

Closing Prayer

Dear God, thank You for the things You give to me. I trust You to provide for me.

Jesus, I love You more than my favorite

_____ .

Thank You for all my blessings.

Parent Page

Jj Job

Dear Parent,

Today your child heard the story of Job. Even when Job lost all he had, he still loved God. We learned that our love for God is not based on the blessings we have been given.

This week try these fun activities with your child:

① Talk with your child about his favorite toys. How can your child show God he loves Him more than his toys?

② Practice generosity. As a family, decide on a favorite item or items you can give away to someone who needs them.

③ Learn Today's Verse: "[Job] said: '. . . The Lord gave these things to me. And he has taken them away. Praise the name of the Lord.'" Job 1:21 ICB

Job

"[Job] said: '. . . The Lord gave these things to me. And he has taken them away. Praise the name of the Lord.'"

Job 1:21 ICB

Jesus Entering Jerusalem
Lesson Theme: Jesus is King.

Materials:

- Palm branches
- Green paint
- Large construction paper

Bible Character: Peter

Bible Verse

"Tell the people of Jerusalem, 'Your king is coming to you. He is gentle and riding on a donkey.'"
Matthew 21:5 ICB

Bible Story

My First Study Bible, pp. 353–58, "Jesus Enters Jerusalem"

Story Application:

- When Jesus entered Jerusalem, some people laid down palm branches for His colt to walk on. They were showing that they loved Jesus and knew He was the Son of God. Other people didn't know Jesus was God's Son. They were not happy Jesus was getting such a nice parade.
- Today we are going to take turns waving the palm branches and saying, "Hosanna" as we parade through the classroom.

Craft

Jesus lived in a place that had palm branches—like California, Arizona, or Florida. So today, we are going to paint with palm branches. Our paintings will remind us of the day Jesus entered Jerusalem.

Dip palm branches in pans of green paint. Then use the palm branches as paintbrushes to paint construction paper.

Closing Prayer

Dear God, thank You that You are my King and I can worship You.

Parent Page

Jj Jesus Entering Jerusalem

Dear Parent,

Today your child heard the story of when Jesus entered the city of Jerusalem and the people waved palm branches before Him.

This week try these fun activities with your child:

1

This week watch a parade. Notice how all the people line up along the sides as the parade goes through the middle of the crowd. That is what it would have been like when Jesus came into Jerusalem.

2

Take a trip to the library and find books with pictures of palm trees. Talk with your child about where palm trees grow.

3

Learn Today's Verse:
"Tell the people of Jerusalem, 'Your king is coming to you. He is gentle and riding on a donkey.'"
Matthew 21:5 ICB

Jesus Entering Jerusalem

"Tell the people of Jerusalem, 'Your
king is coming to you. He is gentle
and riding on a donkey.'"
Matthew 21:5 ICB

Kk King Jesus Dies on the Cross
Lesson Theme: Jesus died for our sins

Materials:
- Red construction paper with heart shape
- Red paint
- Paintbrush
- White chalk
- Scissors

Bible Character: John

Bible Verse

"He was wounded for the wrong things we did . . . And we are healed because of his wounds."
Isaiah 53:5 ICB

Bible Story

My First Study Bible, pp. 412–18, "Jesus Is Crucified"

Story Application:
- Jesus is God, and He is perfect. He never disobeyed His parents or told a lie.
- The only way to be with God in heaven when we die is to be perfect. But we are not perfect. We sin. Because we sin, we cannot live with God.
- Jesus is perfect. When He died, His blood covered our sins so that we could one day be with Him in heaven. When you pray for Jesus' blood to cover your sins, then God does not see your sins. He sees Jesus, and He accepts you just as He accepts His Son, Jesus.

Craft

Have children cut out the red hearts. Pass out the white chalk.

Explain that when we use bad words, disobey our parents, lie, hurt others, etc., we sin against God. That sin hurts our hearts, and we are no longer perfect. Have children draw on hearts.

Jesus' blood washes away our sins and makes our hearts pure again so we can be with God. But for Jesus' blood to wash our hearts clean, we need to agree that we have sinned, pray to Him, and ask Him to come and clean us. We can pray a prayer like this:

"Dear Jesus, I am sorry I am a sinner and I am not perfect. Jesus, You were perfect and You died for me. Please use Your blood to wash my sins away. I love You, Jesus, and I want to be with You and God in heaven one day."

Brush red paint on children's hearts to "wash away" their sins.

Closing Prayer

Dear God, thank You for the gift of Your Son.

Parent Page

Kk King Jesus Dies on the Cross

Dear Parent,

Today your child heard the story of Jesus' death on the cross. We learned that Jesus is God and He is perfect. The only way to be with God in heaven when we die is to be perfect. But we are not perfect. We sin. Because we sin, we cannot live with God.

When Jesus died, His blood covered our sins so that we could one day be with Him in heaven. When we pray for Jesus' blood to cover our sins, God does not see our sins. He sees Jesus, and He accepts us just as He accepts His Son, Jesus.

This week try these fun activities with your child:

1 Tell your child about when you first learned that Jesus died for your sins. Share who told you and how you felt when you heard the story.

3 Learn Today's Verse: "He was wounded for the wrong things we did . . . And we are healed because of his wounds." Isaiah 53:5 ICB

2 This week share with your child when you first prayed and received Jesus' gift of life through His death on the cross.

King Jesus Dies on the Cross

"He was wounded for the wrong
things we did . . . And we are healed
because of his wounds."
Isaiah 53:5 ICB

King Jesus Is Alive!

Lesson Theme: Jesus lives!

Materials:

- Red heart-shaped balloons
- Party helium tank or your own air
- Red strings

Bible Character: Mary

Bible Verse

"Holy, holy, holy is the Lord God All-Powerful. He was, he is, and he is coming." Revelation 4:8 ICB

Bible Story

My First Study Bible, pp. 419–27, "Jesus Is Alive"

Story Application:

- Jesus is alive! Jesus died on the cross and is now alive in heaven with God!
- Do you remember last week when we painted our hearts red? Our sin colored our hearts white, but the blood of Jesus washed them clean again.
- When Jesus rose from the dead, He also gave us another special gift: the gift of the Holy Spirit.

Craft

When Jesus rose from the dead, He "breathed" on the disciples, and the Holy Spirit filled their hearts. When you pray for Jesus to forgive your sins, the Holy Spirit comes in, fills your heart, and helps you to follow Jesus.

Pray with each child:

"Dear Jesus, I am sorry I am a sinner and I am not perfect. Jesus, You were perfect and You died for me. Thank You for Your blood that washes my sins away. I love You, Jesus, and I want to be with You and God in heaven one day. Please send the Holy Spirit to fill my heart."

Explain to the children that we cannot see the Holy Spirit. If we could, it might look like this: Place red heart balloon on helium tank and inflate balloon. Fill one balloon for each child to take home as a reminder of the Holy Spirit, who wants to dwell in their hearts.

Closing Prayer

Dear God, thank You for the gift of the Holy Spirit.

Parent Page

Kk King Jesus Is Alive!

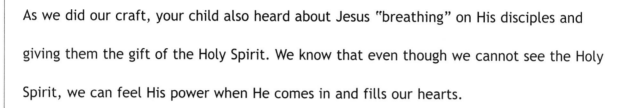

Dear Parent,

Today your child heard the story of Mary Magdalene and the empty tomb.

We learned that Jesus is no longer in that tomb. He's alive!

As we did our craft, your child also heard about Jesus "breathing" on His disciples and giving them the gift of the Holy Spirit. We know that even though we cannot see the Holy Spirit, we can feel His power when He comes in and fills our hearts.

This week try these fun activities with your child:

 1

This week pray for the Holy Spirit to show you something you can do to help someone else in the name of Jesus.

 3

Learn Today's Verse: "Holy, holy, holy is the Lord God All-Powerful. He was, he is, and he is coming."
Revelation 4:8 ICB

2

Listen to a Christian radio station and talk about how many times God is called "Holy" in the songs you hear.

King Jesus Is Alive!

"Holy, holy, holy is the Lord
God All-Powerful. He was,
he is, and he is coming."
Revelation 4:8 ICB

Lazarus

Lesson Theme: Jesus gives new life.

Materials:

- Sunflower seeds
- Small cups
- Potting soil
- Droppers for water

Bible Character: Mary

Bible Verse

"Jesus said to her, 'I am the resurrection and the life. He who believes in me will have life even if he dies.'" John 11:25 ICB

Bible Story

My First Study Bible, pp. 402–11, "Jesus Raises My Brother from the Dead"
Story Application:

- God had the power to bring Lazarus back to life after he died. God also has the power to give you new life.
- Jesus Christ died on the cross so you could ask Him to forgive your sins. When you ask Jesus to come into your life, God gives you a new life just like He gave Lazarus.

Craft

Show the children the seeds you will be planting. Pass them around. Our hearts are hard like these hard seeds. But when we ask God to forgive our sins and come into our hearts, God makes our hearts softer and His love grows inside of us. God's love grows when we read the Bible.

Now we are going to plant seeds to take home. Every time you read the Bible at home, water your seed. As your plant grows, so will the love in your heart that God waters with His Word.

Closing Prayer

Dear God, thank You for sending Your Son, Jesus, so that I may have new life in Him.

Parent Page
Ll Lazarus

Dear Parent,

Today your child heard the story of Jesus raising Lazarus from the dead.

We learned that just as Jesus had the power to bring Lazarus back from the dead, He

also has the power to give us new life in Him.

This week try these fun activities with your child:

(1) Your child planted a hard seed today. As you read the Bible each night, have your child water his plant. As you keep reading and watering, your child will see his plant grow. The growing plant is a reminder to read God's Word each day and will show your child how God's love is growing inside his heart.

(2) Have your child help you plant flowers outside. Take pictures of the small plants and watch them grow through the summer.

(3) Learn Today's Verse: "Jesus said to her, 'I am the resurrection and the life. He who believes in me will have life even if he dies.'" John 11:25 ICB

Lazarus

"Jesus said to her, 'I am the resurrection and the life. He who believes in me will have life even if he dies.'"
John 11:25 ICB

The Lame Man Healed
Lesson Theme: Jesus' name is powerful.

Materials:
- Crown

Bible Character: John

Bible Verse
"Peter said, '. . . By the power of Jesus Christ from Nazareth—stand up and walk!'"
Acts 3:6 ICB

Bible Story
My First Study Bible, pp. 448–53, "A Lame Man Is Healed"
Story Application:
- Peter used Jesus' name to heal the paralyzed man. Jesus' name has power and authority!
- When you are playing with your friends, if they say to you, "Go wash your hands," do you have to go wash your hands? (no) But if your mom says, "Go wash your hands," do you have to go wash your hands? (Yes!) Your mom is an authority over you. You must obey your mom and dad.
- Jesus is the authority over everyone and everything! Jesus is so powerful that even His name has the power to heal.
- Review the rules for the game "Teacher Says." This time, whoever is wearing the crown has the authority and the power to be the "teacher."

Instead of a craft today, play the following game with the children.

Teacher-Says Game (similar to "Simon Says"):
Teacher, give the children directions, but they should obey only if you say, "Teacher says." For example, "Teacher says, touch your feet. (Obey.) Teacher says, wiggle your hands. (Obey.) Touch your nose. (Do not obey—teacher didn't say!)"
Have fun playing this game.

Closing Prayer
Dear God, I praise Your name! God, You are my authority.

Parent Page

LI The Lame Man Healed

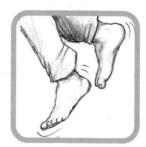

Dear Parent,

Today your child heard the story of the lame man that was healed. We learned that Peter had the authority to heal in Jesus' name.

This week try these fun activities with your child:

1

Let your child be the parent for one hour. He or She can make the rules, but he or she also has to do the parent's chores. Have fun in this role reversal.

2

Talk to your child about the different people in her life who are her authorities and deserve her respect.

3

Learn Today's Verse: "Peter said, '. . . By the power of Jesus Christ from Nazareth—stand up and walk!'"
Acts 3:6 ICB

The Lame Man Healed

"Peter said, '. . . By the power of
Jesus Christ from Nazareth—
stand up and walk!'"
Acts 3:6 ICB

Mm Moses in a Basket

Lesson Theme: We can be adopted by God.

Materials:

- 1 "boat" for each child (paper trays from food-supply stores work best)
- Hay
- Glue
- *The Prince of Egypt* video or DVD
- Baby Moses craft page
- Crayons
- Scissors

Bible Character: Miriam

Bible Verse

"His unchanging plan has always been to adopt us into his own family by sending Jesus Christ to die for us." Ephesians 1:5 TLB

Bible Story

My First Study Bible, pp. 41–47, "God Keeps My Baby Brother Safe"

Story Application:

- After you read the Bible story, watch the beginning of *The Prince of Egypt*. Why did Moses' mom put him in the basket? (to save him) Was he safe? (Yes, because God was watching over him) What did the princess do when she found him? (picked him up and took him home)
- The princess adopted Moses into her family. That means she loved him and took care of him as if he was her own son. Being adopted is very special.
- Did you know Jesus made the way for us to be adopted by God? You can be adopted too! God wants all of us to be His children. To be adopted by God, you need to ask Him to forgive your sins and then ask Jesus into your heart.

Craft

Have children glue hay in their small boats. Color, cut out, and add a paper baby to the boat.

Closing Prayer

Dear God, thank You for being a loving Father.

Parent Page

Mm Moses in a Basket

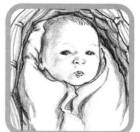

Dear Parent,

Today your child heard the story of Moses being adopted. We learned that God wants all of us to be His children. We become children of God when He adopts us through the blood of His Son, Jesus.

This week try these fun activities with your child:

(1)

Talk to your children about God being their Father.

(3)

Learn Today's Verse: "His unchanging plan has always been to adopt us into his own family by sending Jesus Christ to die for us."
Ephesians 1:5 TLB

(2)

Read *A Blessing from Above*, by Patti Henderson, a story about a kangaroo that adopted a baby birdie.

Moses in a Basket

"His unchanging plan has always been to adopt us into his own family by sending Jesus Christ to die for us."
Ephesians 1:5 TLB

The Island of Malta
Lesson Theme: God has a plan for us.

Materials:
- Map craft page
- Crayons

Bible Character: Paul

Bible Verse
"'I know what I have planned for you,' says the Lord. 'I have good plans for you. I don't plan to hurt you. I plan to give you hope and a good future.'"
Jeremiah 29:11 ICB

Bible Story
My First Study Bible, pp. 480–86, "A Rocky Trip to Rome"
Story Application:
- Paul wanted to go to Rome. God wanted Paul to go to Malta. Instead of screaming and crying and demanding his way, Paul was happy to go to Malta and help the people.
- Paul got to go to Rome just like he wanted. But first he needed to do what God wanted him to do.

Craft
God's plan for Paul's trip was different from Paul's plan. Color the map to see where Paul traveled. Have the children color the water blue and the land brown. Use a red crayon to draw the path that God gave Paul to get him to Rome.

Closing Prayer
Dear God, thank You that You have a plan for my life and it is a good plan.

Rome

Malta

Parent Page

Mm The Island of Malta

Dear Parent,

Today your child heard the story of Paul's shipwreck on the island of Malta.

We learned that Paul wanted to go to Rome, but God needed Paul in Malta first.

This week try these fun activities with your child:

1 Take a local map and use markers to show where your house, child's school, church, and grocery store are.

2 If you take family trips on an airplane, show your child on a map how you would travel by car and how much faster the airplane travels in a straight line.

3 Learn Today's Verse:

"'I know what I have planned for you,' says the Lord. 'I have good plans for you. I don't plan to hurt you. I plan to give you hope and a good future.'"

Jeremiah 29:11 ICB

The Island of Malta

**"'I know what I have planned for you,'
says the Lord. 'I have good plans for you. I
don't plan to hurt you. I plan to give you
hope and a good future.'"**
Jeremiah 29:11 ICB

Nehemiah and the Wall

Lesson Theme: We must pray for God's will.

Materials:

- Clay sticks
- Plastic knives
- Small paper plates

Bible Character: Nehemiah

Bible Verse

"Lord, listen carefully to my prayer. I am your servant . . . Give me, your servant, success today. Allow this king to show kindness to me." Nehemiah 1:11 ICB

Bible Story

My First Study Bible, pp. 228–34, "Rebuilding the City Walls"

Story Application:

- Before Nehemiah asked the king to let him go rebuild the city walls, he prayed to God. When we pray before we do things, we allow God to use us. Because Nehemiah prayed first, he was allowed to go rebuild the walls, and the king even sent help with him.
- God will use you, too! You can pray that God will help you be kind to others, help others, and do what He wants you to do.

Craft

Give each child half a stick of clay and a plastic knife. (Note: Cut the clay stick in half lengthwise. It will be easier for the children to slice into bricks.) Have the children cut the clay into bricks and build a wall to take home.

Closing Prayer

Dear God, when I ask You, please help me to know and do Your will.

Parent Page

Nn Nehemiah and the Wall

Dear Parent,

Today your child heard the story of Nehemiah. Nehemiah wanted to rebuild

the walls of Jerusalem. He prayed to God that the king would show favor to him. The

king not only granted his request, but sent help with Nehemiah!

This week try these fun activities with your child:

1

Have your child ask God for help before he or she gets
ready to do something hard.

2

When we help others, we are helping God. Help your child focus on
helping God by helping others.

3

Learn Today's Verse:
"Lord, listen carefully to
my prayer. I am your ser-
vant . . . Give me, your
servant, success today.
Allow this king to show
kindness to me."
Nehemiah 1:11 ICB

Nehemiah and the Wall

"Lord, listen carefully to my prayer.
I am your servant . . . Give me, your
servant, success today. Allow this
king to show kindness to me."
Nehemiah 1:11 ICB

Jesus Born in Nazareth

Lesson Theme: God became man.

Materials:

- Dinner-size white paper plates
- Gold pipe cleaners
- Light blue triangles of cut paper for angel's body
- Yarn for hair
- Crayons for face
- Glue sticks

Bible Character: Mary

Bible Verse

"For God so loved the world that he gave his one and only Son, that whoever believes in him shall not perish but have eternal life." John 3:16 NIV

Bible Story

My First Study Bible, pp. 310–16, "Jesus Is Born"

Story Application:

- The angels told Mary she would have a baby, and the angels told the shepherds that Jesus was born. God uses angels in the Bible to share important messages from God.
- Jesus' birth was very important. God used His angels to tell people Jesus was here. Today we are going to make our own angels. They aren't real angels, but when we look at them, they will remind us of God's special helpers.

Craft

Before class, cut paper plates into angel shapes using the craft page template. Tape pipe cleaner to the back of the plate and twist into a halo. Have children glue hair and body on angel. Have children color angel's face.

Closing Prayer

Dear God, thank You for sending Your special messengers to tell me Jesus is God.

Parent Page

Nn Jesus Born in Nazareth

Dear Parent,

Today your child heard the story of Jesus' birth. We learned how God sends

angels to share important messages from Him.

This week try these fun activities with your child:

① Talk to your child about the day he or she was born and how you shared the news of his or her arrival with your family and friends.

② Take time to look through your family photo albums with your child. It is so much fun to remember together how much your child has grown!

③ Learn Today's Verse:
"For God so loved the world that he gave his one and only Son, that whoever believes in him shall not perish but have eternal life."
John 3:16 NIV

Jesus Born in Nazareth

"For God so loved the world that he
gave his one and only Son, that
whoever believes in Him shall
not perish but have eternal life."
John 3:16 NIV

Oo Obeying Jesus: Walking on Water
Lesson Theme: We must always keep our eyes on Jesus.

Materials:
- Eyes on Jesus craft page (make 2-sided copies)
- Sunglasses or paper glasses (these may be found at the dollar store)
- Smiley-face stickers

Bible Character: Peter

Bible Verse
"Jesus said, 'Come.' And Peter left the boat and walked on the water to Jesus."
Matthew 14:29 ICB

Bible Story
My First Study Bible, pp. 328–33, "Jesus Walks on the Water"
Story Application:
- When Peter was looking at Jesus, he could walk on the water. When he stopped looking at Jesus and looked at the waves, he got scared and sank.
- We need to keep our eyes on Jesus and follow Him. When we do, we will be able to do all God wants us to do. When we start looking at other people, we will start to "sink," too.
- How do we keep our eyes on Jesus? When we come to church, read the Bible, pray, sing songs to God, worship, and talk to Christian friends and family, we are focusing our eyes on Jesus. Another way to focus on Jesus is to obey His teachings. For example, Jesus taught us to be kind to one another. When we obey Jesus and are kind, we are showing God how much we love Him, and we don't sink by being "mean."

Craft
Today we are going to complete an "eyes on Jesus" activity. On one side, we are going to draw pictures of ways we can keep our eyes on Jesus. (go to church, read the Bible, pray, spend time with friends) On the other side, we are going to draw pictures of things that take our eyes off Jesus. (TV, shopping, fighting)

When they are finished, have the children put on their new glasses and focus on the side of the paper that will help them look toward Jesus. Give each child a smiley-face sticker to put on the Jesus side of his or her paper.

Closing Prayer
Dear God, please keep my eyes focused on You!

Things that keep my eyes on Jesus.

_____

_____

_____

_____

_____

_____

_____

Things that take my eyes off Jesus.

_____

_____

_____

_____

_____

_____

_____

Parent Page

Oo Obeying Jesus: Walking on Water

Dear Parent,

Today your child heard the story of Peter walking on the water to Jesus.

We learned that when we keep our eyes on Jesus, we can do more for God's kingdom.

This week try these fun activities with your child:

(1) Help your child realize when she is "keeping her eyes on Jesus" by helping others, obeying her parents, and reading the Bible.

(3) Learn Today's Verse: "Jesus said, 'Come.' And Peter left the boat and walked on the water to Jesus."
Matthew 14:29 ICB

(2) As a family, talk about what you think Jesus would do in the situations you face daily.

Obeying Jesus:
Walking on Water

**"Jesus said, 'Come.' And Peter
left the boat and walked
on the water to Jesus."**
Matthew 14:29 ICB

Oo The Waves Obey Jesus

Lesson Theme: Jesus calms the storm; nature obeys Jesus

Materials:

- Shaving Cream

Bible Character: Peter

Bible Verse

"Jesus stood up and commanded the wind and the waves to stop. He said, 'Quiet! Be still!' Then the wind stopped, and the lake became calm." Mark 4:39 ICB

Bible Story

My First Study Bible, pp.347–52, "Jesus Calms the Storm"

Story Application:

- Last week we talked about how we can obey Jesus by focusing our eyes on Him. This week we are learning that even nature listens to Jesus!
- Jesus told the wind to stop, and it did! Jesus is VERY powerful! We can trust Jesus to take care of us.
- Who are the strongest people you know? Jesus is stronger! What are the hardest things for you to do? Jesus is strong enough to do all those things!

Craft

Give each child a handful-size blob of shaving cream at his or her spot on the table. Have the children make waves with caps on the lake with their hands. Then have them pretend to be Jesus and make the waves go flat with their hands. Note: Shaving cream washes off quickly and will clean the tables in the process.

Closing Prayer

Dear God, You are awesome and powerful! Even nature obeys You!

Parent Page

Oo The Waves Obey Jesus

Dear Parent,

Today your child heard the story of Jesus calming the storm. We learned that nature obeys Jesus.

This week try these fun activities with your child:

(1)

God is in control of all of nature. During the thunderstorms of spring, remind your child that God is more powerful than the rain and wind.

(2)

Enjoy the breezy days by flying a kite "blown by God."

(3)

Learn Today's Verse: "Jesus stood up and commanded the wind and the waves to stop. He said, 'Quiet! Be still!' Then the wind stopped, and the lake became calm." Mark 4:39 ICB

The Waves Obey Jesus

"Jesus stood up and commanded the wind and the waves to stop. He said, 'Quiet! Be still!' Then the wind stopped, and the lake became calm."
Mark 4:39 ICB

Pp God's Promise to Abraham
Lesson Theme: God keeps His promises.

Materials:
- 2 large paper hearts cut out for each child

Bible Character: Abraham

Bible Verse

"God said to Abraham, '. . . I will bless her. I will give her a son, and you will be the father. She will be the mother of many nations.'"
Genesis 17:15-16 ICB

Bible Story

My First Study Bible, pp. 27–33, "God Kept His Promises"
Story Application:
- God promised two things to Abraham. He promised he would have a son, and he did! Isaac. He also promised that his son Isaac would be the father of many nations. That meant Isaac's children would have many children.
- When God makes a promise, He will do it. God has made you a promise too. If you ask God to forgive your sins and ask Jesus to come live in your heart, God has promised that you have become a child of God and will go to live with Him in heaven one day.

Craft

Do you remember when God put the rainbow in the sky as a reminder of His promise to Noah? God has promised to forgive the things you do that are wrong or bad when you ask Jesus to forgive you. Today we are going to draw a picture on a heart of something you did that was wrong.

After the pictures are drawn, pray with each child for forgiveness for the wrong thing that he or she has done. ("Jesus, I am sorry for _____. Please forgive me, and help me not to sin again.") Take the child's old heart and give him or her a new, clean heart. Asking God to forgive us gives us a new start and cleans our hearts.

Closing Prayer

Dear God, thank You for keeping Your promises! Thank You for promising to forgive me, no matter what.

Parent Page

Pp God's Promise to Abraham

Dear Parent,

Today your child heard the story of God's promise to Abraham. We talked about God's promise to forgive us. Each child drew a picture of something he or she did wrong and prayed for forgiveness. He or she then received a new, clean heart in exchange for the one he or she had drawn.

This week try these fun activities with your child:

1

Promises are very powerful. Promise your child that you will do something special with him or her, like taking a walk together. Be sure to follow through on your promise.

2

Talk with your child about the beautiful plants that are blooming outside. Flowers blooming remind us of the promise of summer coming soon.

3

Learn Today's Verse:

"God said to Abraham, '. . . I will bless her. I will give her a son, and you will be the father. She will be the mother of many nations.'"

Genesis 17:15-16 ICB

God's Promise to Abraham

"God said to Abraham, '. . . I will bless her.
I will give her a son, and you will
be the father. She will be the
mother of many nations.'"
Genesis 17:15–16 ICB

Pp Gods Provision for the 5,000
Lesson Theme: Jesus multiplies food.

Materials:

- Feeding the 5,000 craft page
- Glue sticks
- Scissors
- Crayons
- Construction paper
- 12 loaves of bread (to be donated to the local food bank)

Bible Character: Peter

Bible Verse

"Then he looked to heaven and thanked God for the food . . . All the people ate and were satisfied."

Matthew 14:19-20 ICB

Bible Story

My First Study Bible, pp. 322–27, "Jesus Feeds 5,000"

Story Application:

- How many loaves and fishes did the disciples bring to Jesus? (2 loaves, 5 fishes) How much food did Jesus make? (enough for everyone, with 12 baskets leftover!)
- God is awesome! God will take care of us and provide for us, as He did with the loaves and the fishes.
- God uses the gifts we give Him to provide for others, just as Jesus used the few loaves and fishes the little boy gave Him. In the little boy's hands, it was just enough for his family. In Jesus' hands, it was enough to feed thousands! God multiplies the gifts we give Him of our time, talents, and money.
- To show how much food Jesus created, have a child bring you 2 loaves of bread. Feed each child 1 slice. Then gather up the remaining bread, plus the 10 new loaves. Jesus took not enough food and turned it into enough, with more left over!

Craft

Have children cut out and color pieces on the craft sheet. Have the children glue pieces on craft paper with verse: 2 loaves + 5 fish + Jesus = 5,000 people + 12 baskets of food.

Closing Prayer

Dear God, use me to help You provide for others.

Parent Page
Pp God's Provision for the 5,000

Dear Parent,

Today your child heard the story of Jesus multiplying the fishes and the loaves of bread. We learned that the few loaves and fishes the little boy brought were just enough for his family. In Jesus' hands, it was enough to feed thousands! God multiplies the gifts we give Him of our time, talents, and treasure!

This week try these fun activities with your child:

(1) God provides all we need. Focus this week on the blessings God provides at your house, such as food, warmth, and shelter.

(2) God also provides unexpected surprises, like a clean pair of shorts when you thought they were all dirty. Look for the little provisions God makes in your lives this week.

(3) Learn Today's Verse: "Then he looked to heaven and thanked God for the food . . . All the people ate and were satisfied." Matthew 14:19-20 ICB

God's Provision for the 5,000

"Then he looked to heaven and thanked God for the food . . . All the people ate and were satisfied."
Matthew 14:19–20 ICB

Qq Queen Esther

Lesson Theme: Esther listened for God's will.

Materials:
- Paper crowns
- Sequins, beads, stickers, and markers

Bible Character: Esther

Bible Verse

"Who knows, you may have been chosen queen for just such a time as this."
Esther 4:14 ICB

Bible Story

My First Study Bible, pp. 236–42, "Queen Esther Takes God's Side"

Story Application:
- Esther was afraid to talk to the king, but she also knew she might be able to help her family and friends. Mordecai reminded Esther that God made her the queen so that she could help her family at this time. God had a special plan for her life. But it was her choice whether or not to do God's will.
- God's plan will be done on earth. He gives us the opportunity to be part of His plan. God will give us special ways to help if we look for them.
- Who do you have a special relationship with that you can talk to about Jesus?

Craft

Make a queen's crown. Glue sequins and beads on a paper crown, or let them decorate it using the markers and stickers. Secure the crown to fit each child's head.

Closing Prayer

Dear God, use me in Your plan. Help me do Your will.

Parent Page

Qq Queen Esther

Dear Parent,

Today your child heard the story of Queen Esther. We learned that God

places us in special situations to be used by Him. It is our choice if we allow Him to use

us or not.

This week try these fun activities with your child:

1 We are all children of the "King." That makes us princes and princesses. How would a princess or prince act?

2 Is there some way you know God has placed your family in this city and at this church? Talk to your children about how you feel God is using your family.

3 Learn Today's Verse: "Who knows, you may have been chosen queen for just such a time as this." Esther 4:14 ICB

Queen Esther

"Who knows, you may have been chosen
queen for just such a time as this."
Esther 4:14 ICB

Qq Jeremiah Would Not Be Quiet
Lesson Theme: God's Word is special.

Materials:
- Empty paper-towel rolls
- Paper
- Scissors
- Glue sticks
- Pencils
- Masking tape
- Words of God craft page

Bible Character: Jeremiah

Bible Verse

"This is what the Lord said: 'Jeremiah, stand in the courtyard of the Temple of the Lord. Give this message to all the people of the towns of Judah . . . Tell them everything I tell you to say. Don't leave out any part of my message.'"
Jeremiah 26:2 ICB

Bible Story

My First Study Bible, pp. 259–64, "They Told Me to Be Quiet"

Story Application:
- God gave Jeremiah a list of things to tell the people in Judah. But the people did not want to hear what Jeremiah had to say. The king cut up Jeremiah's list.
- Did Jeremiah stay quiet? NO! Jeremiah wrote another list and sent it to the king again.
- Jeremiah knew that when God tells you to do something, you had better do it!

Craft

Today we are going to make our own scrolls. Using tape, secure each child's paper to his or her paper-towel tube. Then have the children cut out the words of God to glue on their papers. When they are finished, roll up their scrolls to take home. Remind the children to read often how much Jesus loves them!

Closing Prayer

Dear God, thank You for Your Word. I will read it often.

"He has taken our sins away from us as far as the east is from west."
—Psalm 103:12 ICB

"I praise you because you made me in an amazing and wonderful way."
—Psalm 139:14 ICB

"Daniel's God is the living God. ...God rescues and saves people. God does mighty miracles in heaven and on earth."
—Daniel 6:26–27 ICB

"You are a kind and merciful God."   —Nehemiah 9:31 ICB

"All Scripture is given by God and is useful for teaching and for showing people what is wrong in their lives."
—2 Timothy 3:16 ICB

"God decided to to make us his own children through Jesus Christ."
—Ephesians 1:5 ICB

"'I know what I have planned for you,' says the Lord. 'I have good plans for you. I don't plan to hurt you. I plan to give you hope and a good future.'"
—Jeremiah 29:11 ICB

Parent Page

Qq Jeremiah Would Not Be Quiet

Dear Parent,

Today your child heard the story of the prophet Jeremiah. We learned that

even when others do not want to hear the Word of God, we must not be quiet. We must

read the Word of God and keep it in our hearts.

This week try these fun activities with your child:

① Read stories from the Bible together.

② Have your child draw a picture of his or her favorite Bible story to share with a grandparent or friend.

③ Learn Today's Verse:
"This is what the Lord said: 'Jeremiah, stand in the courtyard of the Temple of the Lord. Give this message to all the people of the towns of Judah . . . Tell them everything I tell you to say. Don't leave out any part of my message.'"
Jeremiah 26:2 ICB

Jeremiah Would Not Be Quiet

"This is what the Lord said: 'Jeremiah, stand in the courtyard of the Temple of the Lord. Give this message to all the people of the towns of Judah . . . Tell them everything I tell you to say. Don't leave out any part of my message.'"

Jeremiah 26:2 ICB

Rr
The Redemption of Ruth
Lesson Theme: Ruth was faithful.

Materials:

- Bible Faithfulness craft page
- Crayons
- Envelopes for faithfulness cards
- Stickers, glue, and sequins

Bible Character: Ruth

Bible Verse

"Ruth said, '. . . Every place you go, I will go. Every place you live, I will live. Your people will be my people. Your God will be my God.'"
Ruth 1:16 ICB

Bible Story

My First Study Bible, pp. 115–20, "I Followed God"

Story Application:

- When Ruth's husband died, she could have gone and lived somewhere else. Instead, she chose to stay with her mother-in-law, Naomi. Because Ruth was faithful and stayed to take care of Naomi, God rewarded her with a new husband, Boaz, and baby Obed.
- Ruth received a reward on earth for her faithfulness. People are made glad on earth when we are faithful. We will receive a reward in heaven for our faithfulness.

Craft

Make a Bible faithfulness card. Each child will receive a card with 7 boxes on it. Each box represents a day of the week. Every day that they read their Bible, they can color in that box. Faithfulness means doing something (reading the Bible) every day. Decorate a "faithfulness" card holder with crayons, stickers, and sequins.

Closing Prayer

Dear God, help me to be faithful to You.

Card 1

I am faithful to read
God's word

Monday ☐
Tuesday ☐
Wednesday ☐
Thursday ☐
Friday ☐
Saturday ☐
Sunday ☐

I am faithful to read
God's word

Card 2

I am faithful to read
God's word

Monday ☐
Tuesday ☐
Wednesday ☐
Thursday ☐
Friday ☐
Saturday ☐
Sunday ☐

I am faithful to read
God's word

Card 3

I am faithful to read
God's word

Monday ☐
Tuesday ☐
Wednesday ☐
Thursday ☐
Friday ☐
Saturday ☐
Sunday ☐

I am faithful to read
God's word

Parent Page

Rr The Redemption of Ruth

Dear Parent,

Today your child heard the story of Ruth and her faithfulness to Naomi. We made faithfulness cards to help us remember to read the Bible each day. Our faithfulness is an offering to the Lord.

This week try these fun activities with your child:

1

Help your child remember to read a Bible story every day. Each day he or she does so, help him or her color in a box on his faithfulness card. When the card is full, he or she can bring it to church for a new card.

2

Your child's faithfulness to God's Word is an offering to God. Encourage your child to bring back his or her faithfulness card and put it in the offering bag. It is an offering of his or her time.

3

Learn Today's Verse:
"Ruth said, '. . . Every place you go, I will go. Every place you live, I will live. Your people will be my people. Your God will be my God.'"
Ruth 1:16 ICB

The Redemption of Ruth

"Ruth said, '. . . Every place you go,
I will go. Every place you live,
I will live. Your people will be my
people. Your God will be my God.'"
Ruth 1:16 ICB

The Parting of the Red Sea
Lesson Theme: God performs miracles.

Materials:
- Parting of the Red Sea craft page
- Blue crayons
- Glue
- Paintbrushes
- Dry sand
- A bucket half-full of sand
- Water to wet the sand to saturation

Bible Character: Moses

Bible Verse

"But Moses answered, 'Don't be afraid! Stand still and see the Lord save you today . . . You will only need to remain calm. The Lord will fight for you.'"
Exodus 14:13–14 ICB

Bible Story

My First Study Bible, pp. 57–60, "God Saves My Friends"
Story Application:
- When the Israelites got to the Red Sea, it seemed there was no way for them to escape. God parted the Red Sea for them to escape. God's miracle showed the Egyptians that God was powerful and He could save the Israelites.
- Our God is so awesome! The stories in the Bible tell us of the miracles God has done. God performed a miracle by parting the Red Sea. Not only did God part the water, but He dried up the land so the people and their chariots could drive on it!
- Here is a bucket of sand. (Pour water in it.) This is what the bottom of the sea may have looked like when the water divided. Feel how soft the sand is. Would it be easy or hard to walk on this land? (Hard!)
- God took the water off the top of the sea AND He took the water out of the ground so the people could quickly escape from Egypt. What an awesome God!

Craft

To remind us of how God took the water out of the sea and the land, we are going to color the parted sea and glue sand in the middle for dry land. Teacher, have the children color the sea first and then paint glue in the middle of the sea. Quickly sprinkle dry sand on the wet glue to create a path through the sea.

Closing Prayer

Thank You, God, for showing me Your miracles in the Bible.

Parent Page

Rr The Parting of the Red Sea

Dear Parent,

Today your child heard how God parted the Red Sea for the Israelites to escape from Egypt. We learned that God's miracles are awesome!

This week try these fun activities with your child:

1

Tell your child your favorite miracle story from the Bible.

2

Have your child tell you his or her favorite miracle story from the Bible.

3

Learn Today's Verse: "But Moses answered, 'Don't be afraid! Stand still and see the Lord save you today . . . You will only need to remain calm. The Lord will fight for you.'"
Exodus 14:13–14 ICB

The Parting of the Red Sea

"But Moses answered, 'Don't be afraid! Stand still and see the Lord save you today . . . You will only need to remain calm. The Lord will fight for you.'"

Exodus 14:13–14 ICB

Rahab

Lesson Theme: Hide God's Word in your heart.

Materials:

- Pillsbury crescent rolls
- Small hot dogs
- Cookie sheet
- Toaster oven
- Crayons
- Rahab craft page

Bible Character: Rahab

Bible Verse

"I have taken your words to heart so I would not sin against you." Psalm 119:11 ICB

Bible Story

My First Study Bible, pp. 87–92, "I Chose God's Side"

Story Application:

- Rahab hid the spies under stalks on top of her roof. God allowed the spies to be hidden to save their lives. Later, God allowed Rahab and her family to be hidden to save their lives.
- Today we "hide" the Word of God in our hearts. It is there to help us make good choices for God. We can't see the Bible in our hearts, but we know it is there when we can remember the Bible verses we are learning.
- Make the recipe below for a tasty reminder of how God hid the spies.

Snack

- Open the package of crescent rolls and unroll them.
- In each triangle place a small hot dog.
- "Hide" the hot dog in the dough and place each on a cookie sheet.
- Cook the rolls as directed on the package.
- Enjoy your hidden-surprise treat!

Craft

While you are waiting for the snack to cook, have the children color the Rahab craft page to remind them how God hid the spies.

Closing Prayer

Dear God, help me to learn Your Word and hide it in my heart!

Parent Page

Rr Rahab

Dear Parent,

Today your child heard the story of how Rahab hid the spies. We learned

that we can hide the Word of God in our hearts.

This week try these fun activities with your child:

 1

Tell your child your favorite verse from the Bible.

 2

Practice reading today's verse as a family. See if each of you can memorize the verse before church next week.

3

Learn Today's Verse: "I have taken your words to heart so I would not sin against you." Psalm 119:11 ICB

Rahab

"I have taken your words to heart so I
would not sin against you."
Psalm 119:11 ICB

Samson

Lesson Theme: Friends should build you up.

Materials:
- Paper plate
- Yarn, colored paper, markers, and crayons for faces
- Mirror
- Glue

Bible Character: Samson

Bible Verse
"In this way she began to make him weak. And Samson's strength left him."
Judges 16:19 ICB

Bible Story
My First Study Bible, pp. 106–13, "I Learned to Trust God"
Story Application:
- Remember when we talked about focusing on Jesus? Samson did not focus on God. He was not listening to his godly family and friends.
- Samson's friend was Delilah. Delilah did not believe in God. Soon, Samson told her about his hair. Samson's hair was not the source of his power. God was the source of Samson's power. Not cutting his hair was a way that people could see that Samson had a special relationship with God. When Samson let Delilah cut his hair, it was a symbol that he no longer believed in God's promises.
- We need to have friends who make us better people and help us to focus on God.

Craft
God created each of us to be unique. Just as He did to Samson, God has made a promise to you. You are important to God, and He wants you to be His special child. We are going to make a picture of ourselves to remind us how uniquely God has made us. Teacher, using the mirror, have the children look at their facial features and pick colors for their faces, hair, and eyes. Then have the children glue their faces together.

Closing Prayer
Dear God, help me to be a good friend to others. Help me to choose friends who build me up in healthy ways.

Parent Page

Ss Samson

Dear Parent,

Today your child heard the story of Samson. Samson turned his back on his godly family and friends. We learned that we are special to God and that God wants us to keep our eyes on Him.

This week try these fun activities with your child:

(1)

Encourage your child to share and speak kindly to others.

(2)

Help your child to make good choices in the friends he or she makes.

(3)

Learn Today's Verse:
"In this way she began to make him weak. And Samson's strength left him."
Judges 16:19 ICB

Samson

**"In this way she began to make him weak.
And Samson's strength left him."**
Judges 16:19 ICB

The Thankful Leper

Lesson Theme: The leper was thankful.

Materials:

- Thank-you cards
- Crayons

Bible Character: The Leper

Bible Verse

"Give thanks to the Lord because he is good. His love continues forever."
Psalm 136:1 ICB

Bible Story

My First Study Bible, pp. 379–83, "Jesus Heals Ten Lepers"

Story Application:

- It is easy to forget to thank someone after he or she has helped you. Did you thank your mom and dad today for breakfast, driving you to church, or having clean clothes for you to wear?
- What things can we thank God for? (house, clothes, love, salvation)
- What can we thank Mom and Dad for? (love, clean clothes, food, toys, playing with us)

Craft

Today we are going to make a thank-you card for our moms and dads. We are also going to make a thank-you card for God. Even though we can't hand our cards to God, our cards will be a reminder for us to pray to God and thank Him every day for all the blessings He has given us!

Closing Prayer

Dear God, thank You for all the blessings in my life.

Parent Page
Tt The Thankful Leper

Dear Parent,

Today your child heard the story of the thankful leper. We learned that ten

lepers were healed by Jesus, but only one said thank you.

This week try these fun activities with your child:

Make a game out of saying thank you. Help everyone in your family say thank you to one another for all the big and little things you do each day.

Make thank-you cards and send them to family and friends, thanking them for the gift of friendship they bring to you and your children.

Learn Today's Verse:
"Give thanks to the Lord because he is good. His love continues forever."
Psalm 136:1 ICB

Thank You,
Mom and Dad

Love,

God
Thank You,

Love,

The Thankful Leper

"Give thanks to the Lord because he is good. His love continues forever."
Psalm 136:1 ICB

The Temptation of Jesus in the Desert
Lesson Theme: Jesus withstood temptation.

Materials:
- Bible craft page
- Crayons and markers

Bible Character: Luke

Bible Verse

"Think about the things that are good and worthy of praise. Think about the things that are true and honorable and right and pure and beautiful and respected."
Philippians 4:8 ICB

Bible Story

My First Study Bible, pp. 373–78, "Jesus Is Tempted"

Story Application:

- How did Jesus keep from doing what Satan wanted him to do? (He quoted Scripture.) Jesus told Satan what the Bible said about the things that Satan asked him to do. The Bible can help you too!
- God created the Bible to remind us how to act and what to do when people tempt us. What does it mean to be tempted? (When people try to get us to do things we know are wrong, they are tempting us.) God's Word keeps us from falling into temptation by showing us what is right.
- Philippians 4:8 tells us how we should decide whether or not something is wrong. Let's read the verse and then apply it to some everyday situations.
- Situation 1: "Mom asks you to help her with the dishes." Read the verse. Yes, helping Mom is good. God wants you to do that.
- Situation 2: "Your friend wants you to ride bikes with him, and Mom says that you can." Read the verse. Yes, playing with friends is good.
- Situation 3: "Your friend wants to watch a TV show that Mom said was not very nice." Read the verse. No, God doesn't want you to watch things that are not pleasing to Him.

  Can you see how the Bible can help us every day?

Craft

Hand each child a copy of the craft page and read Philippians 4:8 to the class. Talk about the pictures on the page and how they help you remember the different parts of the verse. Read the verse again to the children and see if they can read the verse with you. Have the children color the craft page. Walk around the room and read the verse with each child while pointing to the pictures.

Closing Prayer

Dear God, thank You for giving me the Bible to help me live my life in a way that is pleasing to You.

Parent Page

Tt The Temptation of Jesus in the Desert

Dear Parent,

Today your child heard the story of how Jesus was tempted in the desert. We learned the Bible verse Philippians 4:8. Philippians 4:8 tells us how we should judge whether or not we should do something. We applied the verse to the following situations in class:

• Situation 1: "Mom asks you to help her with the dishes." Read the verse. Yes, helping Mom is good. God wants you to do that.

• Situation 2: "Your friend wants you to ride bikes with him, and Mom says that you can." Read the verse. Yes, playing with friends is good.

• Situation 3: "Your friend wants to watch a TV show that Mom said was not very nice." Read the verse. No, God doesn't want you to watch things that are not pleasing to Him. This week, use the verse to help your child make wise decisions based on God's Word.

This week try these fun activities with your child:

① Role play different situations with your child using Philippians 4:8 to guide your decisions.

② Take your child out shopping with you and use the setting to talk about temptation. What are you tempted to buy as you walk around the store?

③ Learn Today's Verse: "Think about the things that are good and worthy of praise. Think about the things that are true and honorable and right and pure and beautiful and respected." Philippians 4:8 ICB

The Temptation of Jesus in the Desert

"Think about the things that are good and worthy of praise. Think about the things that are true and honorable and right and pure and beautiful and respected."
Philippians 4:8 ICB

The Temple Solomon Built
Lesson Theme: God's house is special.

Materials:
- Duplo Legos—LOTS of them!
- Ruler with centimeter markings
- Masking tape
- Paper and crayons

Bible Character: Solomon

Bible Verse

"And I will live among the children of Israel in this Temple you are building. I will never leave the people of Israel."
1 Kings 6:13 ICB

Bible Story

My First Study Bible, pp. 215–20, "I Built God's Temple"

Story Application:
- God gave Solomon a pattern for building the Temple. "The Temple was 90 feet long and 30 feet wide. It was 45 feet high" (1 Kings 6:2 ICB). It is hard to imagine how big the Temple was. Remember, Solomon didn't have trucks and other machines to move the stones and wood he needed to make God's Temple!
- Measure and tape off a 90-centimeter by 30-centimeter rectangle on the floor. That will be where you start your walls. Have each child build a stack of 24 Duplo Legos. Place the stacks on the tape and connect them together. Continue until your Temple walls are complete.

Craft
Have the children color their own temples.

Closing Prayer
Dear God, thank You for a place to come and worship You.

Parent Page

Tt The Temple Solomon Built

Dear Parent,

Today your child heard the story of Solomon building the Temple. We learned that God gave special plans for how His house was to be built. We built a smaller temple out of Legos.

This week try these fun activities with your child:

1

Have your child help you fold the laundry. Give specific directions, such as to fold the washcloths in half.

2

Build a tower of blocks with your child. Let him or her tell you which block should go where.

3

Learn Today's Verse:
"And I will live among the children of Israel in this Temple you are building. I will never leave the people of Israel."
1 Kings 6:13 ICB

The Temple Solomon Built

"And I will live among the children of
Israel in this Temple you are building. I will
never leave the people of Israel."
1 Kings 6:13 ICB

U u The Underwater Baptism of Jesus

Lesson Theme: Jesus was baptized.

Materials:

- Styrofoam cups
- Popsicle sticks
- Small picture of each child (such as a school picture)
- Blue crayons
- Tape

Bible Character: John the Baptist

Bible Verse

"Your sins are red like deep red cloth. But they can be as white as snow."
Isaiah 1:18 ICB

Bible Story

My First Study Bible, pp. 366–72, "I Baptized Jesus"

Story Application:

- John baptized people who asked God to forgive their sins. What are sins? (When you break one of God's laws, you sin against God.)
- Because God is perfect, we cannot sin and also live with Him. When God forgives our sins, He makes us clean so that we can live with Him.
- After we pray to God to forgive our sins, He sends the Holy Spirit to come live in our hearts. When this happens, we want to tell the whole world!! We use baptism to show others that God has forgiven our sins and that we are now a part of God's family.

Craft

Each child will decorate a small person and tape the person to a stick. Next, have the children use blue crayons to draw pretend water on the Styrofoam cups. Then insert the stick into the Styrofoam cup. Role play with the children, moving each person under the "water" to baptize him or her.

Closing Prayer

Dear God, thank You for sending Your Holy Spirit to guide me.

Parent Page

Uu The Underwater Baptism of Jesus

Dear Parent,

Today your child heard the story of John the Baptist baptizing Jesus. We learned that being baptized is how we tell others that Jesus has washed us clean from sin by His death on the cross.

This week try these fun activities with your child:

1

Talk to your child about baptism.

2

Go to a celebration and watch people being baptized.

3

Learn Today's Verse:

"Your sins are red like deep red cloth. But they can be as white as snow."

Isaiah 1:18 ICB

The Underwater Baptism of Jesus

"Your sins are red like deep red cloth.
But they can be as white as snow."
Isaiah 1:18 ICB

Vv The Voices Samuel Heard
Lesson Theme: We must listen for God's voice.

Materials:
- Telephone craft page
- Stickers for buttons
- String, scissors, and tape

Bible Character: Samuel

Bible Verse
"Samuel said, 'Speak, Lord. I am your servant, and I am listening.'"
1 Samuel 3:10 ICB

Bible Story
My First Study Bible, pp. 127–33, "I Heard Voices in the Night"
Story Application:
- Samuel heard God talking just as you hear me talking right now. Most people do not hear God so clearly. God talks to us in other ways too! Even though we may not hear God talking, He hears us when we talk to Him. What do we call that? (Prayer!)
- Today we are going to make a pretend telephone. This phone is to remind us of some of the ways we can talk to God. We are going to put 3 buttons on our phone. The buttons say: Bible, church, and prayer. These are 3 different ways we can talk to God and He can talk back to us.

Craft
Have the children cut out their paper phones. Tape a string to attach the receiver to the base of the phone. Then have the children put 3 sticker buttons on their phones. Each button will remind them of a way they can "call" God: Bible, church, and prayer.

Closing Prayer
Dear God, thank You for hearing my prayers.

Parent Page

Vv The Voices Samuel Heard

Dear Parent,

Today your child heard the story of young Samuel hearing God calling him

in the night. We learned we can hear God talk to us through prayer, the Bible, and

attending church.

This week try these fun activities with your child:

①

Encourage your child to pick a different way to talk to God each day this week.

②

Let your child hear you pray to God.

③

Learn Today's Verse: "Samuel said, 'Speak, Lord. I am your servant, and I am listening.'" 1 Samuel 3:10 ICB

The Voices Samuel Heard

"Samuel said, 'Speak, Lord. I am your
servant, and I am listening.'"
1 Samuel 3:10 ICB

The Vessels of Oil
Lesson Theme: God provides the money we need.

Materials:
- Paper Fish craft page
- Clear tape
- Chocolate coins
- Crayons, markers, and scissors

Bible Character: Elisha

Bible Verse
"The thing you should want most is God's kingdom and doing what God wants. Then all these other things you need will be given to you."
Matthew 6:33 ICB

Bible Story
My First Study Bible, pp. 191–96, "I Helped a Widow"
Story Application:
- In this story, God made the widow's oil fill many jars so she could sell them and get money for her family.
- Jesus also helped His disciples get the money they needed. Once when Peter needed money to pay taxes, Jesus told him to go catch a fish. When Peter opened the mouth of the fish, there was a coin inside for Peter to pay his taxes (Matthew 17:24–27).
- We use the money God gives us for many things: keeping our houses warm, buying food, and buying toys. We should be thankful for the gifts God has given us. All His money is precious, and it should not be wasted.

Craft
Have children cut out and decorate 2 paper fish. Tape the 2 fish together around the edges, leaving the mouth open. When the children are finished, have the teacher give each fish a coin.

Closing Prayer
Dear God, help me find my treasure in You.

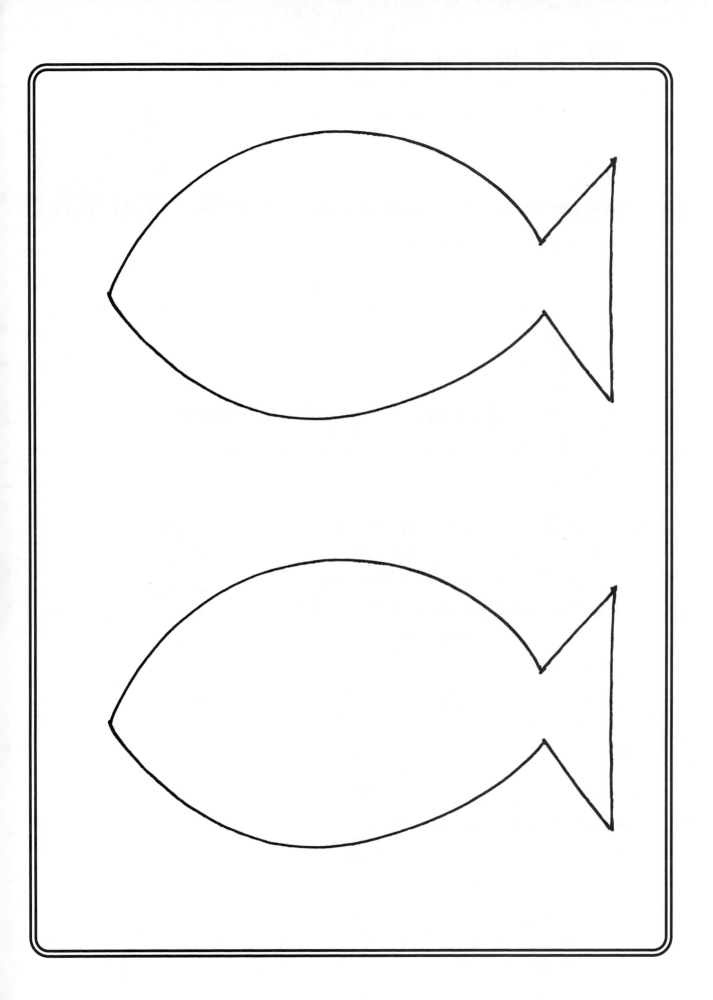

Parent Page

Vv The Vessels of Oil

Dear Parent,

Today your child heard the story of the widow and the vessels of oil that

God filled to provide for her. We learned about treasure.

This week try these fun activities with your child:

Help your child understand that money has value by having him or her help make some choices about what you buy this week. For example: Should we buy gold-fish crackers or graham crackers? Explain that you have enough money for only one item, and he or she can help you choose.

Give your child a set amount of money to buy something to donate to the church.

Learn Today's Verse: "The thing you should want most is God's kingdom and doing what God wants. Then all these other things you need will be given to you." Matthew 6:33 ICB

The Vessels of Oil

"The thing you should want most is God's kingdom and doing what God wants. Then all these other things you need will be given to you."
Matthew 6:33 ICB

Vv The Valley of Dead Bones
Lesson Theme: We will live again.

Materials:

- Dog bones
- Glue
- Heavy-weight paper

Bible Character: Ezekiel

Bible Verse

"And I will put my Spirit inside you. You will come to life."
Ezekiel 37:14 ICB

Bible Story

My First Study Bible, pp. 267–70, "Dead Bones Come Alive"
Story Application:

- The Holy Spirit brings life to our bodies, just as God's Spirit brought life to the bones.
- Our bodies are physically alive, but without the Spirit of God, we are just walking bones. We need the Holy Spirit to fill us up and help us follow God.

Craft

Have fun making people out of dog bones. Glue the bone people to heavy-weight paper.

Closing Prayer

Dear God, thank You for the gift of Your Holy Spirit.

Parent Page

Vv The Valley of Dead Bones

Dear Parent,

Today your child heard the story of the prophet Ezekiel, who spoke the

words God told him to say and brought a valley of dead bones to life. We learned that we

are just walking bones without the gift of life the Holy Spirit gives.

This week try these fun activities with your child:

 1

Try to fly a kite on a windless day. Then try to fly a kite on a windy day. God's Spirit moves like the wind. We cannot see it, but it is very powerful.

 2

Visit a museum and look at the bones of dinosaurs and other animals that once were alive but are now dead. Talk about what it would have been like to live with dinosaurs!

 3

Learn Today's Verse:
"And I will put my Spirit inside you. You will come to life."
Ezekiel 37:14 ICB

The Valley of Dead Bones

"And I will put my Spirit inside you. You will come to life."

Ezekiel 37:14 ICB

Ww
The Whale That Ate Jonah
Lesson Theme: We need to obey God.

Materials:
- Bible pieces to retell story
- Plastic zipper bags

Bible Character: Jonah

Bible Verse
"Honor your father and your mother." Exodus 20:12 ICB

Bible Story
My First Study Bible, pp. 292–99, "I Learned to Obey God"
Story Application:
- Jonah was given a job to do that he didn't want to do. Do you ever have jobs you don't want to do? Jonah needed to obey God, just as we need to obey our moms and dads.
- Eventually Jonah did obey God and told the people what God wanted them to hear. However, he had to be stuck in a fish before he did what God told him to do!
- Now retell the story using the story pieces.

Craft
Today we are going to make story pieces so we can retell the story of Jonah and the whale to our families and friends. Cut out Jonah, the whale, the people, and God. Have the children follow along, using their story pieces, as you read the story again. When you are finished, put the Bible pieces in a plastic zipper bag for each child to take home.

Closing Prayer
Dear God, I will obey my mom and dad.

Parent Page

Ww The Whale That Ate Jonah

Dear Parent,

Today your child read the story of Jonah being swallowed by the whale. We

learned that Jonah disobeyed God, and God allowed the whale to swallow him.

This week try these fun activities with your child:

(1)

Thank your child every time he listens to you as his
parent. The more he can obey you, the more he will be
able to obey God's Word. Teach him that obeying his
parents is a part of obeying God.

(3)

Learn Today's Verse:
"Honor your father and
your mother."
Exodus 20:12 ICB

(2)

Set up a tent and pretend it is
the belly of the whale that
swallowed Jonah.

The Whale That Ate Jonah

"Honor your father and your mother."
Exodus 20:12 ICB

The Water in the Rock

Lesson Theme: Our words are powerful.

Materials:

- Small cans or jars with lids
- Beans
- Paper cut to fit around jar
- Markers
- Tape

Bible Character: Moses

Bible Verse

"Shout to the Lord, all the earth. Serve the Lord with joy. Come before him with singing."
Psalm 100:1–2 ICB

Bible Story

My First Study Bible, pp. 73–78, "I Disobeyed God"

Story Application:

- Did you notice that the people in the story were complaining? The Israelites complained a lot! Do you ever complain and whine to your mom and dad? What do they say when you whine?
- Let's all whine, "I want a snack." (Everyone whines.) Now stop. How did that sound to your ears? Now let's all say in a nice voice, "I would like a snack, please." (Repeat phrase.) If you were Moses, which way would you want to hear people asking for food?
- Moses disobeyed God. God said to speak to the rock, but Moses hit the rock. Do you think if the people were not complaining that Moses would have hit the rock? How you ask for things and how you talk to people affects how they talk to others.
- One of the best ways to cheer someone up or change a bad mood is to sing. God loves to hear our songs. They are music to His ears. Today we are going to make music sticks to remind us to sing a joyful song to God!

Craft

Have each child decorate a paper strip with markers. Fill each child's jar one-third full of beans. Tape the paper around the outside of the jars. Use shakers while singing the children's favorite worship songs.

Closing Prayer

Dear God, thank You for filling my heart with joy!

Parent Page

Ww The Water in the Rock

Dear Parent,

Today your child heard the story of Moses' disobedience to God. We learned that the people were whining and complaining to Moses. We are going to try to ask for things without whining and cheer people up by singing worship songs.

This week try these fun activities with your child:

①

Turn on the radio, dance, and sing to change your mood while cleaning the house.

②

Thank your child when he or she makes requests without whining. Share how it makes you feel when he or she asks for help in a nice way.

③

Learn Today's Verse: "Shout to the Lord, all the earth. Serve the Lord with joy. Come before him with singing." Psalm 100:1-2 ICB

The Water in the Rock

"Shout to the Lord, all the earth.
Serve the Lord with joy. Come
before him with singing."
Psalm 100:1–2 ICB

The **W**hirlwind That Took Elijah
Lesson Theme: God is powerful.

Materials:

- Plastic jar with lid
- Monopoly houses
- 3 drops liquid dish-washing detergent
- Whirlwind craft page copied on 80# paper for each child

- Strings, 50 inches long
- Jar of white liquid glue
- Bucket of water for children to wash hands

Bible Character: Elijah

Bible Verse

"Then Elijah went up to heaven in a whirlwind." 2 Kings 2:11 ICB

Bible Story

My First Study Bible, pp. 183–90, "God Brought Me Home in Style"

Story Application:

- Elijah was taken to heaven in a whirlwind. Today, tornados and hurricanes are the closest things we can think of that would resemble a whirlwind. Both are destructive and bring fear and heartache. God used the whirlwind of the Old Testament as a happy thing to bring Elijah quickly to God in heaven.
- God's ways are not our ways. Think about God's awesome power and how He can use every thing for good as you watch this whirlwind.
- Teacher to create a whirlwind: Fill the jar three-quarters full with water. Put 3 drops of liquid soap and a few monopoly houses in the jar. Screw the lid on tight. Shake the jar 15 times and then twist the jar in your hand. Watch the whirlwind take shape in the bottle.

Craft

Now we are going to make a whirlwind to take home. Dip your string in glue until the whole string is covered. Lay your string on the whirlwind shape, starting at the bottom.

Closing Prayer

Dear God, I am in awe of Your power. Please keep me safe.

Parent Page

Ww The Whirlwind That Took Elijah

Dear Parent,

Today your child heard the story of Elijah being taken to heaven in a whirl-wind. We learned that God is powerful.

This week try these fun activities with your child:

(1)

Talk about tornado and hurricane safety and where you would go in an emergency.

(2)

Go to the library and check out books about tornados and hurri-canes.

(3)

Learn Today's Verse: "Then Elijah went up to heaven in a whirlwind." 2 Kings 2:11 ICB

The Whirlwind That Took Elijah

"Then Elijah went up to heaven in a whirlwind."
2 Kings 2:11 ICB

Zaccheus
Lesson Theme: Jesus forgives.

Materials:
- Bible pieces to retell story
- Plastic zipper bags

Bible Character: Zaccheus

Bible Verse
"Happy is the person whose sins are forgiven, whose wrongs are pardoned."
Psalm 32:1 ICB

Bible Story
My First Study Bible, pp. 389–95, "I Saw Jesus"
Story Application:
- Zaccheus was a sinner. Remember, a sinner is someone who breaks God's laws. Did that mean that God didn't love him? NO! God loves everyone! When Zaccheus brought Jesus to his house, he asked Jesus to forgive him. Did Jesus? YES! Remember, Jesus loves you too! Whatever we do wrong, Jesus will forgive us if we ask Him to.
- Now retell the story using the story pieces. Have the children cut out and color their own story pieces and retell the story with you before they go home.

Craft
We are going to make story pieces so we can retell the story of Zaccheus to our families and friends. Cut out Zaccheus, the tree, Jesus, the house, and Zaccheus's money bag. (The love of money was his sin.) Have the children follow along as you read the story again using their story pieces. When you are finished, put the Bible pieces in a plastic zipper bag for each child to take home.

Closing Prayer
Dear God, thank You for loving me and forgiving my sins.

Parent Page
Xx, Yy, Zz Zacchaeus

Dear Parent,

Today your child heard the story of Zacchaeus. We learned that Jesus loves us even when we sin. Jesus will always forgive us when we ask Him to.

This week try these fun activities with your child:

1

Zacchaeus learned that he had to ask for forgiveness. Help your child ask for forgiveness when he or she misbehaves or makes a poor choice.

2

If the opportunity arises, ask your child for forgiveness!

3

Learn Today's Verse: "Happy is the person whose sins are forgiven, whose wrongs are pardoned."
Psalm 32:1 ICB

Zacchaeus

"Happy is the person whose sins are
forgiven, whose wrongs are pardoned."
Psalm 32:1 ICB

Wrap-Up Week 1

Lesson Theme: Rainbows remind us of God's promises.

Materials:

- Rainbow-circle cereal
- Yarn
- Construction paper in rainbow colors
- Pencil
- Scissors
- Tape

Bible Verse

"I have placed my rainbow in the clouds as a sign of my promise." Genesis 9:13 TLB

Bible Story

My First Study Bible:

"God Kept Me Safe," pp. 21–26

"God Makes Good from Bad," pp. 34–39

Story Application:

- God used the rainbow to show Noah that He would never flood the land again.
- Joseph's coat showed him how special he was to his dad.
- Today we are going to make a rainbow for our room and a rainbow to wear to remind us of God's promises to us.

Craft

First, have children trace and cut out their hands on construction paper of different colors. Tape hands up in a rainbow on the wall. Next, have children string rainbow-circle cereal on yarn to wear home.

Closing Prayer

Dear God, thank You for Your promises to me.

Parent Page

A–Z Celebration! Wrap-Up Week 1

Dear Parent,

Today your child reread the stories of Noah's ark and Joseph's rainbow coat. We focused on rainbows, talking about God's promises to us and how special we are to Him.

This week try these fun activities with your child:

1 Let your child finger paint with red, blue, and yellow paint. What new colors of the rainbow does he or she make?

2 Cut 1-inch squares of tissue paper, and have your child glue them to a plastic lid. What happens when the colors overlap? Punch a hole in the lid, and hang it in your kitchen window.

3 Learn Today's Verse: "I have placed my rainbow in the clouds as a sign of my promise." Genesis 9:13 TLB

A–Z Celebration!
Wrap-Up Week 1

"I have placed my rainbow in the clouds as a sign of my promise."
Genesis 9:13 TLB

Wrap-Up Week 2

Lesson Theme: Fire is used in the Bible to show God's presence.

Materials:

- Red, orange, and yellow crepe paper cut in 8-inch strips
- Empty paper-towel rolls (1 for each child)
- Tape
- Electric fan

Bible Verse

"There the angel of the Lord appeared to Moses in flames of fire coming out of a bush. Moses saw that the bush was on fire, but it was not burning up."
Exodus 3:2 ICB

Bible Story

My First Study Bible:

"God Teaches Pharaoh a Lesson," pp. 48–56

"Shadrach, Meshach, and Abednego," pp. 272–78

"I Tell People About Jesus," pp. 441–47

Story Application:

- God used fire in the burning bush to talk to Moses.
- God used an angel in the fiery furnace to protect Shadrach, Meshach, and Abednego.
- God sent the Holy Spirit to earth like little tongues of fire.

Craft

Today we are going to make our own fire logs. Tape strips of crepe paper to the empty paper-towel rolls. Have children place their log in front of the fan to show how the fire dances in the wind.

To reenact the story of the burning bush, take the children outside and have them put their fire on a bush, but the bush does not burn.

To reenact the story of Shadrach, Meshach, and Abednego, have the children stand in two rows fanning their flames. Pick three children at a time to walk through the flames and not be hurt.

Closing Prayer

Dear God, thank You for showing me Your power in the fire.

Parent Page

A–Z Celebration! Wrap-Up Week 2

Dear Parent,

Today your child reread the stories of Moses and the burning bush;

Shadrach, Meshach, and Abednego; and the Holy Spirit. We talked about how God has

used fire to reveal Himself to us.

This week try these fun activities with your child:

①

Watch the Veggie Tales movie *Rack, Shack, and Benny* as a family.

②

Read stories by the fire (in the winter) or outside by a fire pit (in the summer) and enjoy the warmth.

③

Learn Today's Verse: "There the angel of the Lord appeared to Moses in flames of fire coming out of a bush. Moses saw that the bush was on fire, but it was not burning up." Exodus 3:2 ICB

A–Z Celebration!
Wrap-Up Week 2

"There the angel of the Lord appeared to Moses in flames of fire coming out of a bush. Moses saw that the bush was on fire, but it was not burning up."
Exodus 3:2 ICB

Wrap-Up Week 3

Lesson Theme: God's gift of grace is Jesus.

Materials:

- Red construction paper heart for each child
- Crayons

Bible Verse

"For God so loved the world that he gave his one and only Son, that whoever believes in him shall not perish but have eternal life."

John 3:16 NIV

Bible Story

My First Study Bible:

"Jesus Is Born," pp. 310–16

"Jesus Is Crucified," pp. 412–18

"Jesus Is Alive!" pp. 419–27

Story Application:

- God sent Jesus to the earth to save us from our sins. Jesus led a perfect life.
- Jesus died on the cross. His blood covers our sins. When we pray for Jesus' blood to cover our sins, God sees Jesus' perfect life instead of our sins.
- When Jesus rose from the dead, He came to give us a special gift. He gave us the gift of the Holy Spirit. The Holy Spirit guides us and helps us to do God's will on the earth.

Craft

Help each child write something that he or she is thankful for on the paper heart. Have the children sit in a circle. As you walk around the circle behind each child, thank God out loud for what he or she has written, and then have all the children say, "Thank you, Jesus!"

Closing Prayer

Dear God, thank You for the gifts of Jesus and the Holy Spirit.

Parent Page

A–Z Celebration! Wrap-Up Week 3

Dear Parent,

Today your child reread the stories of Jesus' birth, death, and resurrection.

We talked about God's gift of salvation through Jesus, and the gift of the Holy Spirit.

This week try these fun activities with your child:

1

Share with your child how much Jesus means to you. Encourage him or her to share Jesus with someone.

2

Imagine what life would be like if you did not know Jesus.

3

Learn Today's Verse: "For God so loved the world that he gave his one and only Son, that whoever believes in him shall not perish but have eternal life." John 3:16 NIV

A–Z Celebration!
Wrap-Up Week 3

"For God so loved the world that he gave his one and only Son, that whoever believes in him shall not perish but have eternal life."
John 3:16 NIV

Master Materials List for *The ABC's of the Bible*

A is for Adam and the Apple
* Apple wedges for snack
* Red, green, and yellow apples
* Red, green, and yellow paint
* Paintbrushes
* Construction paper
* Knife to cut apple

A is for Noah's Ark
* Cool Whip
* Small plates and spoons
* Round rainbow cereal
* Animal stickers (2 for each animal)
* Parachute or large golf umbrella
* Cotton balls
* Rainbow craft page
* Crayons
* Glue

B is for Blessings to Hannah
* Paper and crayons

B is for the Boy King
* Josiah craft page
* Yellow, red, and brown crayons for each child

C is for the Children Jesus Loves
* Magazine pictures of children
* Large paper heart
* Sticker hearts (1 for each child)
* Paper people
* Wiggly eyes, yarn, and paper to glue on
* Glue

C is for the Coat of Many Colors
* Coffee filters
* Spray bottle filled with water
* Washable bold-tip markers
* Paper towels

D is for David and Goliath
* Tin foil cut for each child
* Construction paper
* Glue sticks

D is for Daniel and the Lions' Den
* Animal crackers for snack
* Animal crackers for craft
* Construction paper
* Glue

E is for Elijah
* A slice of bread for each child
* 2 cups oil
* 12 cups flour
* 2 cups water
* Large bowl and wooden spoon
* Plastic zipper bags

E is for the Egyptian Plagues
* Bowl
* Whole milk
* Food coloring
* Dish soap

F is for Faith in the Fiery Furnace
* Tissue-paper squares cut out of red, orange, and yellow tissue paper
* Glue sticks
* Fire craft page
* Blindfold

F is for Freedom from Chains
* 80# copy paper cut into one-inch strips (two for each child)
* Crepe paper
* Stapler
* Choir robe for teacher
* Tape

G is for Grace Given to Peter
* Sugar cookies with sprinkles for snack
* Empty toilet-paper rolls
* 2 4-inch squares of clear cellophane or wax paper for each child
* 2 cups rice mixed with glitter
* White construction paper cut to 3 x 4 inches to go around toilet-paper roll
* Tape

G is for Gideon
* Construction paper cut to bookmark size
* A piece of fleece
* Stickers, crayons, and markers to decorate bookmarks

H is for Healing the Paralyzed Man
* Get-well cards copied on colorful copy paper
* Stickers, crayons, and markers to decorate cards
* Lunch bags to store cards (1 for each child)

H is for the Holy Spirit Sent to the Disciples
* Holy Spirit craft page
* Red, yellow, and orange paint
* Paintbrushes
* Gold glitter

I is for I Worship Jesus
* Worship God craft page
* Crayons and markers

J is for Joshua in Jericho
* Sugar cubes
* Small paper plates
* Glue (not glue sticks)
* Large building blocks or shoeboxes

J is for Job
* Crayons
* Job craft page

J is for Jesus Entering Jerusalem
* Palm branches
* Green paint
* Large construction paper

K is for King Jesus Dies on the Cross
* Red construction paper with heart shape
* Red paint
* Paintbrush
* White chalk
* Scissors

K is for King Jesus Is Alive!
* Red heart-shaped balloons
* Party helium tank or your own air
* Red strings

L is for Lazarus
* Sunflower seeds
* Small cups
* Potting soil
* Droppers for water

L is for the Lame Man Healed
    * Crown

M is for Moses in a Basket
    * 1 "boat" for each child (paper trays from food-supply stores work best)
    * Hay
    * Glue
    * *The Prince of Egypt* video
    * Baby Moses craft page
    * Crayons
    * Scissors

M is for the Island of Malta
    * Map craft page
    * Crayons

N is for Nehemiah and the Wall
    * Clay sticks
    * Plastic knives
    * Small paper plates

N is for Jesus Born in Nazareth
    * Dinner-size white paper plates
    * Gold pipe cleaners
    * Light blue triangles of cut paper for angel's body
    * Yarn for hair
    * Crayons for face
    * Glue sticks

O is for Obeying Jesus: Walking on Water
    * Eyes on Jesus craft page (make 2-sided copies)
    * Sunglasses or paper glasses (these may be found at the dollar store)
    * Smiley-face stickers

O is for the Waves Obey Jesus
    * Shaving cream

P is for God's Promise to Abraham
    * 2 large paper hearts cut out for each child

P is for God's Provision for the 5,000
    * Feeding the 5,000 craft page
    * Glue sticks
    * Scissors
    * Crayons
    * Construction paper
    * 12 loaves of bread (to be donated to the local food bank)

Q is for Queen Esther
    * Paper crowns
    * Sequins, beads, stickers, and markers

Q is for Jeremiah Would Not Be Quiet
    * Empty paper-towel rolls
    * Paper
    * Scissors
    * Glue sticks
    * Pencils
    * Masking tape
    * Words of God craft page

R is for the Redemption of Ruth
    * Bible Faithfulness craft page
    * Crayons
    * Envelopes for faithfulness cards
    * Stickers, glue, and sequins

R is for the Parting of the Red Sea
    * Parting of the Red Sea craft page
    * Blue crayons
    * Glue
    * Paintbrushes
    * Dry sand
    * A bucket half-full of sand
    * Water to wet the sand to saturation

R is for Rahab
    * Pillsbury crescent rolls
    * Small hot dogs
    * Cookie sheet
    * Toaster oven
    * Crayons
    * Rahab craft page

S is for Samson
    * Paper plate
    * Yarn, colored paper, markers, and crayons for faces
    * Mirror
    * Glue

T is for the Thankful Leper
    * Thank-you cards
    * Crayons

T is for the Temptation of Jesus in the Desert
* Bible craft page
* Crayons and markers

T is for the Temple Solomon Built
* Duplo Legos—LOTS of them!
* Ruler with centimeter markings
* Masking tape
* Paper and crayons

U is for the Underwater Baptism of Jesus
* Styrofoam cups
* Popsicle sticks
* Small picture of each child (such as a school picture)
* Blue crayons
* Tape

V is for the Voices Samuel Heard
* Telephone craft page
* Stickers for buttons
* String, scissors, and tape

V is for the Vessels of Oil
* Paper Fish craft page
* Clear tape
* Chocolate coins
* Crayons, markers, and scissors

V is for the Valley of Dead Bones
* Dog bones
* Glue
* Heavy-weight paper

W is for the Whale That Ate Jonah
* Bible pieces to retell story
* Plastic zipper bags

W is for the Water in the Rock
* Small cans or jars with lids
* Beans
* Paper cut to fit around jar
* Markers
* Tape

W is for the Whirlwind That Took Elijah

* Plastic jar with lid
* Monopoly houses
* 3 drops liquid dish-washing detergent
* Whirlwind craft page copied on 80# paper for each child
* Strings, 50 inches long
* Jar of white liquid glue
* Bucket of water for children to wash hands

X, Y, Z is for Zacchaeus

* Bible pieces to retell story
* Plastic zipper bags

A-Z Celebration! Wrap-Up Week 1

* Rainbow-circle cereal
* Yarn
* Construction paper in rainbow colors
* Pencil
* Scissors
* Tape

A-Z Celebration! Wrap-Up Week 2

* Red, orange, and yellow crepe paper, cut in 8-inch strips
* Empty paper-towel rolls (1 for each child)
* Tape
* Electric fan

A-Z Celebration! Wrap-Up Week 3

* Red construction paper heart for each child
* Crayons

About the Author

Lisa Woodruff has a passion to make the Bible come alive for children of all ages. She holds a bachelor's degree in education from Miami University and is a contributing writer to *Magnify, the New Testament Biblezine for Kids* (Tommy Nelson). Lisa lives in West Chester, Ohio, where she loves being a busy mom to Joey and Abby and spending quality time with her husband, Greg.

Max Lucado presents . . .

Come along with Max Lucado's fun-filled Hermie and Friends™, and dive in and discover God's gift for you. Using six great themes of the Bible, *Splash!* is a comprehensive lesson plan for children ages 3-8. As the children go to the W-E-L-L, they will learn of Jesus' Work, Energy, Lordship, and Love!

- Includes a CD-Rom with fully reproducible materials
- Includes craft ideas, activity sheets, coloring pages, memory verse games and songs

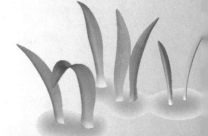